ST. ALBERT
THE GREAT

ST. ALBERT THE GREAT

CHAMPION OF FAITH AND REASON

Kevin Vost, Psy.D.

TAN Books
Charlotte, North Carolina

ISBN: 978-0-89555-908-1

Cover design by Milo Persic.

Cover image: Albertus Magnus © Brother Lawrence Lew, O.P.

Printed and bound in the United States of America.

TAN Books
Charlotte, North Carolina
www.TANBooks.com
2011

To Sister Mary Lawrence Green, O.P.
and the Dominican Sisters of Springfield, Illinois

Contents

PART III
LOVER

Acknowledgments

> Great men are not great for themselves alone; they bear
> us up; our confidence is implicitly grounded in their exis-
> tence. With their help, we can make for ourselves a life
> as great as theirs, except for the disproportion between
> our powers and theirs.
>
> —A. D. Sertillanges, O.P.[1]

M Y first and foremost thanks go out to Todd Aglialoro, my four-
time editor, and therefore a paragon of the virtues of patience
and perseverance, four times over. Many thanks as well to all at TAN
Books who agreed it was time again to tell the story of Albert the
Great, such a great-souled though unsung saint.

Also duly acknowledged are those dynamic people in the world
of Catholic media who afford me the joy of sharing the messages
within my books. These include, to name but a few, John Barger
at Sophia Institute Press; Bert Ghezzi of Our Sunday Visitor; Matt
Swaim and Brian Patrick of EWTN/Sacred Heart Radio's Son Rise
Morning Show; Dave Zelzer and Wendy Wiese at Relevant Radio;
Leslie Teeling and Jon Leonetti at KWKY Catholic Radio Des
Moines; Al Kresta and Nick Thomm of Kresta in the Afternoon; and
Darin DeLozier and Patrick Coffin at Catholic Answers Live. Many
thanks also to Johnnette and Thea Benkovic, two Women of Grace at
EWTN, and also to Doug Keck and Lee South, who have featured my
previous books on the EWTN Bookmark show.

Among the many great-souled individuals I've had the pleasure to
collaborate with recently in various projects and endeavors, special
thanks to authors Shane Kapler, Peggy Bowes, and Cheryl Dickow;

blogger/reviewer Steven McEvoy; Katy Walker of iibloom.com, and to psychotherapist Karen Rumore. Thanks so much for recommending my books of old (though they're not that old).

Finally, thanks as always to Kathy Vost, who so deftly runs a family and a household, while I plod along at a book-laden desk and a keyboard.

A Great Man for All Seasons

> Magnanimity by its very name denotes stretching forth
> the mind to great things . . . And since a virtuous habit
> is denominated chiefly from its act, a man is said to be
> magnanimous chiefly because he is minded to do some
> great act.
>
> —St. Thomas Aquinas[2]

> They [scientists] need courage and initiative in their efforts
> to fathom the secrets which nature holds, and to adapt their
> discoveries to the needs of man: that requires magnanimity,
> which was Albert's most characteristic quality.
>
> —Sr. M. Albert, O.P.[3]

TOO few today are truly great. We've become a culture of nar
row chests, sloped shoulders, and shrunken heads. And my,
what tiny noggins! It seems we just aren't putting enough substantial
stuff inside our brains to keep them from shriveling back inside their
vacant vaults. No wonder so few of us wear hats today, what with so
little cranium to hold them up. We are awash in information, plugged
in constantly to electronic media, yet our attention is scattered. Nothing sinks in. What flies in the one ear, flies right out the other, leaving
a passage for the next fleeting little sound bite of useless trivia.

There is much truth to a commonplace saying of our day: "Use it or
lose it!" We're just not using our minds enough to stop the shrinkage,
and we've allowed ourselves to become small, small as individuals

and small as a culture. We've become a "culture of death" because we think too small to embrace the bigness and greatness that is life.

So what do we need to become great, to achieve that quality of magnanimity or "greatness of soul" of which St. Thomas Aquinas speaks? We need a hero.

We need the witness of people who have become, by the grace of God, great. People who have taken their God-given talents and gifts and run with them. People whose lives, as St. Thomas put it, "savor of excellence."[4]

St. Thomas certainly knew firsthand about greatness of soul. His mind was always stretched toward the greatest of all things—God and also to His creation as it reflected Him. He also studied intently and wrote copiously on this concept of magnanimity, basing his work largely on the efforts of Aristotle, who had stretched his mind like no other before and very few since. And he also had the acquaintance of one of those very few men who were actually called "great" while they still lived on Earth. That man was St. Thomas's teacher, and later, the champion of his thought. He is the subject of this book: St. Albert the Great.

St. Albert stretched his entire being toward many great things. He was "broad of shoulders," "noble in body and mind," with "a wonderful memory for fact."[5] His life savored of excellence in so many different areas. With the eye of the scientist, he plumbed the secrets of nature; with the heart of a saint, he never forgot that nature was Creation. He was grateful to God and to all the living and the dead who had taught him and helped him. He was beneficent and generous like few others, sharing his plenitude of gifts not only with the men and women of his time, but with those of our time and all times.

Please join me, then, as I lay out a plan for stretching our minds toward the life and lessons of this great-souled man, the professor of the University of Paris, the German provincial of the Order of Preachers, the bishop of Ratisbon, the patron of the sciences, the Universal Doctor of the Catholic Church: St. Albert the Great.

Introduction

The Least Shall Be the Greatest

> They had discussed with one another who was the greatest. And he sat down and called the twelve: and he said to them, "If any among you would be first, he must be least of all and servant of all."
>
> —Mark 9:34–35

> St. Albert can fittingly be called the miracle and wonder of our time.[1]
>
> —Ulric of Strasbourg

THOUGH he wasn't canonized until 1931, St. Albert of Cologne has been known as "the great" since his own day—the 13th century—due to his incredible breadth of knowledge. It was said that Albert quite simply knew everything there was to know! Throughout these pages, then, we'll look at how he put his powerful mind to plumbing the mysteries of creation through virtually every science and intellectual discipline known to man—literally from "a" to "z," with contributions to fields as diverse as anatomy, anthropology, astronomy, biology, botany, chemistry, dentistry, geography, geology, medicine, physiology, physics, psychology, and zoology.

Albert was a master philosopher as well, intimately conversant with the systems of the most profound thinkers of the ancient Greek and Roman worlds. In his mastery of scripture and theology, also, he knew few peers in his time. And Albert did not keep his knowledge to himself. He was a great professor, teaching philosophy and the sciences to grateful students throughout Europe. For these reasons, and good reasons they are, Albert was called "great" in his own time.

Perhaps you are wondering, though, "If Albert was so great, then why don't *we* know more about him?" Good question! And the answer, I think, is found in those words of Jesus that began this introduction. It is one thing to be great in the eyes of the world, still another to be great in the eyes of Christ. Albert had *both* kinds of greatness, and it was because of that second, Christlike kind of greatness that he did not seek to draw attention to himself. He did such a good job making himself the least and servant of us all that the world has, in some measure, forgotten his true stature.

We'll see in the pages ahead how St. Albert has been compared by saints and sages, by professors and by popes, to great men such as King Solomon, St. Luke, St. Paul, and St. Ambrose. But to demonstrate here his understated greatness, I draw your attention to those who have compared him to that voice crying in the wilderness, St. John the Baptist. St. John was a blessed man who devoted himself entirely to God's works and displayed unmatched humility before Him who was to follow. Like the blessed Baptist who prepared the way for the Lord, so too St. Albert prepared the way for another: the man would become that great defender and lover of Jesus and most profound teacher of the doctrines of Christ's Church, the Angelic Doctor, St. Thomas Aquinas.

Indeed, today perhaps the one thing that most everybody knows about St. Albert is that he was St. Thomas's teacher, the man who helped groom the most exquisite mind ever to serve the Church. As the famous story (which I'll retell later) goes, St. Albert promised that the "bellowing of this ox [that is, the words of St. Thomas], would be heard around the world!" Today it appears that St. Albert's prophecy has rung so true that the bellowing of that blessed ox has inadvertently drowned out the life and lessons of his own great teacher!

Thus, today there is a relative dearth of recent material on Thomas's great teacher. In preparing to write this book, I searched the Web sites of the Catholic publishers and booksellers, the major secular bookstores, and even the Library of Congress. I certainly may have missed some, but the most recent biography I could find on St. Albert was written in 1955—and that's a fictionalized tale geared toward adolescents.[2]

Other biographies I found, tracked down through obscure and out-of-the-way booksellers, were written in 1948, 1938, 1932, and 1876.[3] Those 20th-century books came out shortly after Albert was canonized and declared a Doctor of the Church in 1931 and declared the patron saint of the sciences in 1941, and they also highlight his lessons for those living in that era in modern history. I was pleased to see that some new books addressing various aspects of Albert's thought have become available to English-language readers in recent years, and I'll tell you about them in the relevant chapters ahead. But all in all I could see that it was past time for a new book about St. Albert the Great, one that explained his life and virtues for the general reader of today. Here's the basic game plan for it.

The Life, the Legend, the Lessons

This book is biographical in part. I'll share the many significant events of St. Albert's life, and in an appendix I'll even throw in (at no extra charge) a chronology of his life and his influence since his death. Still, in writing a biography of a man so great, and a man who lived so long ago, it becomes difficult at times to separate fact from fiction. As with other saints of centuries past, a great number of pious stories have accrued to Albert's name over the centuries, and as with any saint, it is not always easy to ascertain their veracity. Specifically to St. Albert, many questionable *scientific, technological, architectural,* and indeed, even *magical* stories have accrued to his great name as well!

Historians have weighed in on the reasons in favor of believing or disbelieving some of these amazing stories, and I'll try to let you know when we've moved from the pretty well-established facts of the "life" to the more questionable stuff of the "legend," in case it is not obvious. And no, I'm not going to share any of these wonderful tales right now. You'll simply have to read along (or skip ahead), but

I do want to make a point about these legends.

Though I am unable to separate the wheat of fact from the chaff of fancy in some of these tales (I'd need the help of St. Albert himself for that), here is a question I'd like us to chew on. If people were someday to craft legends about *you* and *your life*, what might they be? What would you *like them* to be? In St. Albert's case, whether some of these events happened as told or not, we can't say for certain; that these stories *have* been told, of that we can be sure. Further, both the life *and* the legend carry for us important lessons, and those lessons are the main reason for this book. Since he was a teacher and preacher to the core, I feel sure that the great saint himself would want it that way.

THE ROLES OF VIRTUES

We'll see in chapters ahead (especially Chapter 12) that our hard-nosed scientist-saint had a soft spot in his heart for our Mother Mary. In his writings on the Blessed Virgin, he emphasized that in being "full of grace,"[4] Mary possessed *all* the virtues and graces available to a human being and personified their perfection. Albert himself was no stranger to the virtues. He wrote complete philosophical and theological works on what virtues are and how to build them. As we examine his life, we will contemplate the multiple virtues that made up the character of this great saint, so that we too might try to grow in like virtues of our own.

Ancient philosophers like the ancient Greek Epictetus and Roman Seneca (St. Albert knew them well) urged us toward lives of virtue, noting that when we desire nothing more than virtue, we will attain great peace, becoming relatively undisturbed by the misfortunes and difficulties that we all encounter. Attaining this inner tranquility is one of the hallmarks of the Stoic sage or wise man. But these were enterprising Greeks and Romans, mind you, not navel-gazers; for the Stoics, once the virtuous soul attains control over his own passions, the question follows, "Now what shall I *do*?"

Epictetus in particular was wont to answer that we should play the roles the great "Playwright" has assigned to us—be it the role of a citizen, a brother, a sister, a son, a daughter, a father, a mother, a student, a teacher, a soldier, an official—whatever the case may be. In other words, our virtues will be displayed and shared when we perform our work and our duties to others as human beings. Indeed, virtues themselves grow and thrive through their exercise in the active roles we are called to play in the service of God and our fellow man.

As we will soon see, Albert was a man of nearly as many roles as virtues. The Great One was no mere bookworm (or "noodle" as my father-in-law was prone to call the intellectually inclined). The great scholar and teacher was also provincial of his religious order for the entire province of Germany, a bishop of a diocese, a Vatican advisor, and even a preacher of a Crusade—and his virtues shined forth in every role.

GREAT IDEAS

We'll examine virtues themselves, as St. Albert saw them, in some detail in Chapter 4. For now, let me simply note that virtues themselves are *embodiments of excellence*. They are perfections of human powers. They are also ideas, in the sense that we can't directly see or touch or hear or taste or smell things like courage or humility or justice or kindness, but we can indeed come to know them, experience them, display them, and share them through the use of our intellects and our wills. That's why each and every chapter of this book will end with a "Great Ideas" section, each focusing on a particular virtue embodied by Albert himself in the subject area of that chapter. I'll provide definitions, highlight Albert's examples, and offer practical suggestions for making these great ideas our own.

THINKER, DOER, LOVER

The chapters of this book are organized into three parts, based on three parts of the famous motto of the Dominicans (St. Albert's order):

"To share with others the fruits of contemplation." The Dominicans sought to study deeply the things of God and creation, and then to preach them, so as to save men's souls.

Part I, "Thinker," will highlight St. Albert's role as an intellectual giant in science and philosophy, that which brought him fame and the title "the great" in his own time. Thinking also ties in most directly to the Dominican call to study and contemplation. Further, thinking calls for virtues of its own—like understanding, wisdom, and even science—*intellectual* virtues St. Albert knew and lived so well.

In Part II, "Doer," I'll highlight St. Albert as the man of *action*. St. Albert wasn't the type to "just think about it," no, he was also the type to "git 'er done!" Here we'll see him move from the ivory tower out into the street, as the professor becomes spiritual shepherd to a diocese, as the author of learned treatises becomes the author of peace treaties between warring parties, as the preacher to the novices becomes the preacher of a great Crusade to the Holy Land in defense of Christian Europe. Doing has its virtues too, *natural* or *moral* virtues, and here we'll see just how St. Albert's contemplation bore a bumper crop of natural fruits.

When St. Paul proclaimed the highest class of virtues, the God-infused *theological* virtues of faith, hope, and love, he told us the highest was love.[5] Jesus had told us after all that the greatest commandment of all is to love the Lord our God with all that we are, and the second is to love our neighbor as ourselves.[6] St. Albert knew these commands quite well and obeyed them like few others. And as a spiritual son of St. Dominic, he knew as well that those fruits of contemplation were meant *for sharing with others.* In Part III, "Lover," then, we will examine the true heights of Albert's greatness, the ways that he showed his love of God, God's Mother, his fellow religious, and his students.

And just about last, near the end of the day (or at least near the end of this book), we will see how before his death, and after a lifetime of service, he who was so great became again like the least, as the light of his memory and intellect dimmed. But we'll also see how the fire of his passion for God burned bright until his last day as a traveler on this earth.

Finally, we'll see how, 650 years after his death, the Catholic Church made official what those who knew him knew all along, that Albert was not only great but a saint, and a Doctor—the Universal Doctor—of the Church. His truly was one of the greatest human minds God has given to the universe. So it's darn well time we get to know him better by sitting at his great feet.

PART I

THINKER

Chapter 1

Saintly Scientist

The first [cause], God—the most true, most sweet, most
powerful from eternity forever and ever and reigning
through boundless ages—can be known in another way,
that is, through his effects.

—St. Albert the Great[1]

I recommend to you particularly the virtues of courage, which defends science in a world marked by doubt,
alienated from truth, and in need of meaning; and humility, through which we recognize the finiteness of reason
before Truth which transcends it. These are the virtues of
Albert the Great.

—Pope John Paul II[2]

PERHAPS you've heard the tale from history books about how
Europe was cast in darkness after the fall of Rome. About how
it then endured centuries of "dark ages" and only slightly brighter
"middle ages" until the bold humanists of the Renaissance cast off
the mental shackles of the Catholic Church; rediscovered the wisdom
of the ancient pagans; and brought a rebirth of vitality, science, and
intelligence to all the Western world.

Well, I'd like to tell two little stories of my own, the first from one
of those very Renaissance men, Francis Bacon (1561–1626).

In the year 1432, a group of scholars had been tirelessly and fiercely
debating a question of grave importance for a period of nearly two
weeks. They had consulted a vast array of ancient learned texts (no

doubt the esteemed works of Aristotle and the Church Fathers among them) but could find no answer to their dilemma. The mystery itself was that of "the number of teeth in a horse's mouth," but alas, none of the ancient wise men had addressed it and thus arose their stalemate.

Well, on the 14th day, a young friar in their company (I suspect a Dominican) asked if he might make a suggestion, which was to go out into the barn and look into the open mouth of a horse and count the teeth. The scholars were "sore vexed" at such a ludicrous suggestion "in a manner so coarse and unheard-of." Thereupon, they fell upon the young man, "smote him hip and thigh," and kicked him out. When they had calmed down and regained their composure many days later, one of them declared the problem an "ever-lasting mystery," since none of the great theologians had ever addressed it, and "so ordered the same writ down."[3]

That's some funny stuff—and told so well in Bacon's own words. But before I make any comment, let's consider the other story.

On a cold Christmas Eve, 13 centuries after the birth of Our Lord, two young German brothers stole from their beds and trod stealthily toward the family barn, hoping to avoid notice of the watchman pacing upon the stone walls. In a land of many tales, the boys had been told that on the eve of Christ's birth, the animals of the stable spoke as humans did. The older brother speculated that the ox might say, "'O-o-o-omnes'—that means 'all'—'Come all ye faithful.'" The younger brother, only seven, had feared that the animals might speak in Latin, in which case his big brother would have to translate for him. In any event, as they sunk down in the hay and began to observe the ox, the younger brother sneezed; a groomsman heard it, found the boys, and brought them back inside. The younger brother apologized for the sneeze but assured his brilliant older brother that he was so smart that undoubtedly that ox would have spoken just as he thought, since "you're always right about those things!" But the big brother shook his head and said, "I want to know for *sure* . . . I want to *hear* them—and then we'll know. You can't always go by what people say."[4]

I came across Bacon's story of the medieval scholars in a history of psychology class I took in 1993, and it has never failed to amuse me;

but as my own knowledge of history and psychology grew, it began to annoy me a bit as well. Bacon presents quite the caricature, portraying the learned doctors of the Middle Ages as unfamiliar with—and flat out opposed to—knowledge of the natural world. That was certainly not always the case, most especially among the friars who wore the habit of St. Dominic!

The second story, the one about the little boys, I came across in *Master Albert*, Sister Dorcy's children's book on St. Albert the Great. The big brother who insisted that he wanted to know *for sure* would one day be known as the consummate medieval scholar: Albertus Magnus, Albert the Great! The events of that tale, by the way, would have taken place more than 200 years before Bacon's little fantasy.

Even if *both* tales are fictional, one thing we'll learn from the life and lessons of St. Albert is that long before the Renaissance, learned men of God had turned the light of their intellects to the natural world as well, and, like God Himself, they declared it good, very good!

On Albert's Nature

Albert was a consummate naturalist. He was enamored of created things, from the literal birds and bees to flowers, spiders, lizards, dogs, mountains, stones, and stars, from a very early age. But as immersed as he was in the cultural and spiritual milieu of the medieval age, he knew the things of nature were not complete ends in themselves. He saw nature as the handwork of God that also mirrored, though imperfectly, the nature of its Creator.

One of the myriad natural subjects to interest St. Albert was that of individual differences. What makes each one of us unique? He sought answers in the ancient science of *physiognomy*, which sought to examine traits of human character, especially as revealed in facial features. Let's imagine, if you will, the faces of three great saints, and see what they might tell us.

St. Albert was a member and a leader of the Dominican order, whose preacher-friars traveled great distances by foot throughout all of Europe. If we could look upon the face of St. Dominic himself as he walked along, we might well find him looking down or straight ahead, immersed in prayer or conversing about God with his religious brothers. St. Thomas Aquinas, another saintly Dominican, was famous for his professorial absent-mindedness, unaware of his physical surroundings as he pondered the deepest philosophical and theological mysteries. We'd likely see a far-away stare in his eyes. But St. Albert we would probably see walking with his eyes wide open, looking all around him at the wonders of creation. In fact, it's said that young Albert was so distracted from his spiritual studies by his love of nature that the Virgin Mary, the "Seat of Wisdom" herself, had to come to him to set him straight.

ALBERT ON NATURE

St. Albert wrote extensively on the natural world, with books specifically addressing plants, animals, minerals, and more. I've seen only snippets of most of them, but I've been able to acquire a new English translation of his *Questions Concerning Aristotle's On Animals.*[5] Here, in 19 "books," or what we would call chapters, Albert addresses a total of 442 questions on an amazing (and sometimes amusing) diversity of subject matters. Here is a small sample of questions, to give you but a taste of the breadth of his concerns. Some of these may seem rather odd and archaic today and some, perhaps, surprisingly timely:

- Book One, Question 19: Why some animals have feet and some do not.
- Book One, Question 26: Why eyebrows that are straight indicate femininity and pliability whereas ones arched toward the nose indicate discretion and intellect.
- Book One, Question 43: Why a human has such a large brain size in proportion to his body size.
- Book Two, Question 3: Whether the right foot is more unfettered and better suited for motion than the left.

- Book Two, Question 27: Whether the human ought to lack a tail naturally.
- Book Three, Question 27: Whether the marrow is necessary for the bone's nourishment.
- Book Four, Question 6: Whether fish have hearing.
- Book Four, Question 21: Why some people who eat more are thin, whereas others who eat only a little are fat.
- Book Seven, Question 32: Whether pestilential disease arises from an infection of the air.

Here Albert seeks to know the nature and workings of all varieties of animals and of man himself, both inside and out. He seeks to understand the anatomy and habits of fish, birds, camels, and horses, as well as the mysteries of human conception, growth, development, and aging. He ponders the quirky anomalies of the human mind, covering issues as far-ranging as why "madmen" have such great physical strength to why wise men seem prone to having frivolous children. Albert's fascination with and love for all of creation burst forth from every page.

Here is a morsel of special significance to me, because on many a day I have sat in a little swivel rocker, swilling coffee, reading books about St. Albert while one of these little guys peered quizzically at me, just feet away, from his perch on a little tree just outside my picture window. "The pirolus is an extremely lively little animal; it nests in the tops of trees, has a long bushy tail, and swings itself from tree to tree, in doing so it uses its tail as a rudder. When on the move it drags its tail behind it, but when sitting it carries it erect up on its back. When taking food it holds it as do the other rodents in its hands, so to speak, and places it in its mouth. Its food consists of nuts and fruit and such-like things."[6] He goes on to describe how its coloring varies in Germany (black when young), in Poland (reddish gray), and in Russia (gray). I'd call the ones in my own neighborhood reddish brown, though there are lots of little gray ones in a park just two miles away.

Perhaps you have identified the "pirolus." I always associate them with that other great saint of nature, St. Francis of Assisi. For me, this may be partly due to that little statue right outside the same window. One rests at Francis's shoulder while a deer and a rabbit flank his sides. Now though, whenever I see a busy little squirrel, I think of both a great Franciscan *and* a great Dominican saint!

Albert was a wonderful observer and describer of nature. Observation and description are the key elements to a scientific approach to the world, after all. When I taught college psychology, I told my students that the three key goals of psychological research were (1) *to describe* the domain of observational research, (2) *to explain* the domain of experimental research, and (3) *to optimize* the domain of practical application. I'm going to attempt to show in the pages ahead how, though rare for the 13th century, Master Albert was a master of all three.

ALBERTUS MAGNUS, SCIENTIST

Some in Albert's own time considered him a dangerous innovator, potentially drawing pious souls toward philosophy and science and thereby, they reasoned, away from God. Others in his day and in centuries since have considered him a magician, so vast was his knowledge of nature, mechanics, and medicine. Still others, however, in the centuries after his death, and up to the present day, have considered Albert too little the scientist, chastising him for his ostensible gullibility and his close dependence on Aristotle and other ancients. This last is the kind of thing we saw in the tale of Francis Bacon that began this chapter.

Which is it? If the scientist's goal is to find the truth, based on the evidence, then to find the truth on St. Albert's role as a scientist we need to go to the evidence available to us: St. Albert's own writings and achievements.

Some critics have charged that St. Albert followed Aristotle—who made many errors in his writings on science and nature—too uncritically.

But Albert himself pointed out that Aristotle was human and prone to errors. For one example, Aristotle had written that the lunar rainbow occurred only once every 50 years, but Albert reported that Aristotle was in error because he had seen two in the same year himself! And in another instance, where Aristotle had noted that eels feed on nothing but slime, Albert corrects him by noting that he had seen for himself eels feasting on the likes of frogs, worms, and fish. Albert also corrected Aristotle on the number of human ribs and other things.

In reading St. Albert's purely scientific writings, we likewise find errors and gaps in knowledge common to the greatest minds of his day. Sometimes his sources were responsible for the errors (Albert would often qualify in his writings if certain events had only been reported to him rather than be observed with his own eyes). But often he would set about to verify or correct those very sources with his own experiments. It had been reported, for example, that ostriches ate iron pellets, so he tested this and found an ostrich had no taste for them. He had heard that cicadas continued to produce their noise after they'd lost their heads, which he tested and found to be true. In these and other simple experiments and comments, he showed that he did indeed display a true scientific mindset—one guided by evidence, by observation, and where possible, by experiment.

Indeed, should a modern scientist consider St. Albert's understanding of the nature and spirit of the scientific mindset lacking, I would direct him, for a start, to Book 11 of the aforementioned *Questions Concerning Aristotle's On Animals*. The very first question is "Whether there is a double mode of proceeding in science."[7] By "double mode" he refers to two of the same major goals of science I explained to my college students more than 700 years after St. Albert: "one descriptive, and the other assigning causes," that is, to describe and to explain the provinces of observational and experimental research.

But St. Albert does far more than name them. In his analysis of science as proposed by Aristotle, Albert examines deeply the very nature of observation and of experimentation, noting how observation serves as a necessary starting point to show us the "whats" of nature, while experiment can lead us to the "whys" as well. He analyzes the four great classes of causes (material, formal, efficient, and final), the nature of scientific classification, including the use of genus and species, and so much more, showing true depth of understanding. He also displays something too often lacking in modern scientists: science's own dependence on philosophy. Philosophy defines the laws of logical reasoning that we apply to scientific observations and experimental findings, both to find truths about the material world and to help us understand the limitations of those findings.[8]

Though many of his findings have been superseded by modern science, with its instruments and technologies far exceeding those of seven centuries ago, Albert helped end a scientific standstill that had lasted about three centuries before his time, and his grasp of the very heart of science remains illuminating even today.

Below is a small sample of a few of Albert's specific scientific contributions with regard to observation, classification, and predictive theory:

- He isolated arsenic.
- He provided the first description of the spinach plant in Western writing.
- He did early work in the theory of protective coloration of animals—including the prediction that animals in the extreme north would have white coloring.
- He determined that the Milky Way is a huge assemblage of stars.
- He determined that the figures visible on the moon were not reflections of earth's mountains and seas but features of the moon's own surface.
- He predicted land masses at the earth's poles.
- He predicted a large land mass to the west of Europe.
- He determined, with the use of mathematical formulae, that the earth was spherical.[9]

COURAGE AND HUMILITY

There is no doubt that Albert was a scientist, and in his day a great one. But the true greatness of the saintly scientist today shines forth in his saintliness. For him, science served as a means to understand God through His creation, to deepen our awareness of His majesty in the glorious wonders of the universe that is His handiwork. Saints, of course, are models of virtue, and two virtues ascribed to St. Albert by another man whom people have begun to call "the Great," Pope John Paul II, are the virtues of *courage* and *humility*.

The quotation that heads this chapter was found in a speech that John Paul II gave in Cologne, Germany, on November 15, 1980, on the 700th anniversary of the great saint's death. November 15 is the feast of St. Albert, Cologne is one place where Albert taught, and the speech was given to university professors and students. I find this little speech interesting in part because it serves as a preview in miniature to John Paul's great encyclical of 18 years later, *Fides et Ratio*.

John Paul II exhorted his audience to the kind of *courage* that Albert had displayed. In his day Albert was blasted by some who believed that science threatened the Christian worldview. But Albert knew well though, as John Paul would state eloquently many centuries later, that faith *and* reason are the two wings on which we fly to the truth. Albert also had the courage to speak out boldly against those who spoke out against science, even within his own Dominican order: "There are those ignorant people who wish to combat by every means possible the use of philosophy, and especially among the preachers, where no one opposes them; senseless animals who blaspheme that of which they know nothing."[10]

St. Albert's courage to seek the Truth was complemented and perfected by his humility in seeking the Truth, as well. In the words of John Paul II, "Man's reason is a grand instrument for knowledge and structuring of the world. It needs, however, in order to realize the whole wealth of human possibilities, to open to the Word of eternal Truth, which became man in Christ."[11]

For St. Albert, the instrumental power that derives from scientific knowledge of the world was not a means to move away from God, or to make man a god, but a way to better conform man to God's image. John Paul II notes that science can lead to great advances for the benefit of mankind and should be pursued wholeheartedly. Still, science cannot give us *meaning*, and science alone cannot guarantee respect of *human dignity*. For these things we need more than mastery of the material world. We also need "science" in its older, broader meaning: the rational, systematic study of any subject matter, including theology, that "divine science" that examines God, the ultimate source of all subject matters. Christian theology, as Albert, Thomas, and John Paul II have told us, stands on twin pillars of reason and faith, of science and revelation. It is in his deep understanding and love of God that St. Albert's true greatness, born of humility, shines through.

In the chapters ahead, we'll go back to the beginning, examining Albert's own life from the days of the youthful falconer, to the days of the great man of knowledge and of action, to the last days of the elderly child of God, waiting patiently to see his Father face-to-face. We'll see how this scientist-saint, this teacher-preacher, this lover of creation and Creator can inspire us to grow in our own love and knowledge as well.

GREAT IDEA #1: THE VIRTUE OF SCIENCE

In his papal address of March 24, 2010, Pope Benedict XVI drew the world's attention to St. Albert the Great as a model for the modern scientist to follow in transforming the study of nature into a fulfilling and "fascinating journey of holiness." Pope Benedict spoke of the "friendship" of reason and faith, of St. Albert's realization that reason and scripture are completely compatible, and of God's will that we use both to seek and attain Truth and happiness.

So amazing were some of Albert's actual scientific accomplishments in the 13th century that they gave rise to some pretty fascinating legends, most portraying him as a kind of magician. One tale tells of how Albert "made summer in winter," when King William of Holland called to visit Albert in the dead of winter, and Albert entertained him and his party in a plush summer garden. (Albert had most likely crafted an early greenhouse.) In another story, St. Thomas stumbles on the statue of a beautiful young woman behind a curtain in Albert's laboratory. After the statue greets him in a human voice, *"Salve, salve, salve!"* the startled, gentle giant destroys it, proclaiming, "Begone, Satan!" St. Albert then comes in and chides his young apprentice for destroying the work of 30 years. This would suggest, though we can't say for sure, that Albert had produced a human doll or robot or sorts, capable of producing speechlike sounds—predating Chatty Cathy by 700 years!

And now for more serious matters. Building on the ideas found in Aristotle's *Nicomachean Ethics* and other writings, St. Albert wrote about the three *intellectual virtues* of *understanding, science,* and *wisdom. Understanding* is the grasp of principles, the comprehension of universal concepts and essences of things. It bespeaks the rational or intellectual soul, possessed only by humans among all creatures on Earth. *Science* derives from the Latin *scio,* meaning "to know." The virtue of science refers to intellectual excellence in grasping the nature of causes and effects. *Wisdom* is the ultimate intellectual virtue, standing on the twin pillars of understanding and science and casting judgment on both the conclusions of science and the principles on which they are based.[12] Wisdom is the stuff of philosophy and theology, subjects in which Albert too was very "great."

The scientists of today who can find in the universe no room for God have a far too narrow view of the essence of science, assuming that what we can know includes only those material things we can quantify and measure, ignoring the reality of the spirit and of human experience and meaning. They live in a cramped, soulless world and would do well to seek out the Truth to be found in the life and the lessons of a great-souled scientist.

Chapter 2
Studious Student

Albert had an insatiable thirst for truth, a patient tireless energy of inquiring into natural phenomena, a vivid
imagination joined to a tenacious memory, a sane esteem
for the established wisdom of the past.

—Pope Pius XI[1]

Albert asked for a comprehensive knowledge of human
learning. The holy Virgin granted his petition, promising
that no one should surpass or equal him in learning.

—Marianus M. Vetter, O.P., D.D., Ph.D.[2]

A LBERT was born in AD 1193, or 1206, or perhaps we could
split the difference and say about 1200. As is not uncommon
for even notable personages of the Middle Ages, we have no firm
documentation of the date of Albert's birth. Early biographers, seiz-
ing on a statement that Albert died in 1280 at the age of 87, calculate
his year of birth as 1193. A plaque on a tower commemorating the
house of his family in his hometown of Lauingen bears the 1193
date as well.[3] Other historians point to multiple testimonies reporting
his entry into the Dominican order in 1222 at age 16 and deduce he
was born in 1206. "Circa 1200" was the choice of James Weisheipel,
both an Albertine scholar and the definitive biographer of St. Thomas
Aquinas,[4] and we too shall proceed with that approximate date. This
way, as we progress through the chronology of his life, we should
never be more than six or seven years off in estimating Albert's age
at the time of his great thoughts and deeds.

Perhaps it is providential that we have much more extensive documentation of Albert's lessons than of the details of his life. Surely he would have preferred it this way. Although in some later writings, in particular his commentary on the Gospel of St. Luke, he hearkens back to fond memories of his youth, we have no record of anything approaching an autobiography. Still, despite the dearth of information on Albert's early life, we'll unearth what we can as we focus on his education.

On the Blue Danube

Albert was born in Lauingen, a small town on the left bank of the Danube River in Bavarian Swabia, near the city of Ulm, and in the diocese of Augsburg. Lauingen today is a town of about 11,000 residents in southeastern Germany. It lies about 150 miles to the west of another Bavarian town, Marktl am Inn, the birthplace of another notable German theologian, known to us today as Pope Benedict XVI.

Albert came from a family of lower nobility, of the class called the "militaries." This title implied no direct military role but indicated service to the emperor of the House of Hohenstaufen and representation of the emperor's power in one's own locality. Ancient documents describe Albert's father as a cavalier or as an officer of the Royal Court, and Albert's uncle appears to have served in a similar capacity. In any event, Albert's family possessed the stately nearby castle of Bollstadt, and we will see that Albert will refer to this castle as a model for fortifications in his later writings.

We know for sure that Albert had a young brother, Henry (the other little boy in search of talking animals from the fictionalized tale of our last chapter). He, too, became a Dominican friar, was the prior of the convent of Visburg, and is named in Albert's will. Tradition holds that Albert also had a sister who became a Dominican nun, partly because in his will he also made a bequest to a Dominican convent in Swabia, where she may have still been living at the time of his death. So, too, and for the same reason, is there speculation that he had another sister, a nun of the convent of St. Catherine at Augsburg. Documents from the 13th and 14th century regarding his family indicate that Albert had other brothers as well and the male line of his family can be traced until its extinction in 1607.

Of Albert's early life, we have only snippets of recollections in his later writings. Sister Dorcy delightfully portrays young Albert as a boy with a passion for nature, falconry in particular. Albert's writings show extensive knowledge of all kinds of nature's wonders, from the varieties and behaviors of birds and animals of the forest to the varieties of fish in the Danube. Indeed, it has been said that you could repopulate the forests of Bavaria with the creatures discussed within his books. We saw above that Pope Pius XI spoke of Albert's "tireless energy of inquiring into natural phenomena"; and his mastery was so great, we can safely conclude that this energetic inquiry began very early on in the great saint's youth. But what of the early formal education that would lay the foundation of the man who would know almost all there is to know? To this question we turn next.

SEVEN WAYS TO A GREAT EDUCATION

In 1947, the mystery writer and Christian apologist Dorothy Sayers produced an essay titled "The Lost Tools of Learning," which bemoaned how products of current educational methods seemed especially inept at seeing through propaganda, resisting the claims of advertising, and separating fact from opinion and truth from falsity in the messages of mass media. Sayers wrote of the power of the press and of radio to mold the minds of the poorly educated: "By the invention of the film and the radio, we have made certain that no aversion to reading shall secure them from the incessant battery of words, words, words. They do not know what the words mean; they do not know how to ward them off or blunt their edge or fling them back; they are a prey to words in their emotions instead of being the masters of them in their intellects."[5] As an antidote, Sayers prescribed time-tested educational methods that can equip young students to grow into adults who can think for themselves, who can reason and see through false arguments, who can carefully define the terms with which they speak and argue, who can recognize there is a truth to be sought, and who can know what it takes to seek it. So how does this tie in to the 13th-century education of Albert of Lauingen? It was to his era that Sayers looked for her antidote:

> What, then, are we to do? We cannot go back to the Middle Ages. That is a cry to which we have become accustomed. We cannot go back—or can we? . . . I should like every term in that proposition defined. Does "go back" mean a retrogression in time, or the revision of an error? The first is clearly impossible per se; the second is a thing which wise men do every day. "Cannot"—does this mean that our behavior is determined irreversibly, or merely that such an action would be very difficult in view of the opposition it would provoke? Obviously the twentieth century is not and cannot be the fourteenth; but if "the Middle Ages" is, in this context, simply a picturesque phrase denoting a particular educational theory, there seems to be no a priori reason why we should not "go back" to it—with modifications—as we have already "gone back" with modifications, to, let us say, the idea of playing Shakespeare's plays as he wrote them, and not in the "modernized" versions of Cibber and Garrick, which once seemed to be the latest thing in theatrical progress.[6]

Let us "go back," then, and investigate how Albert's teachers taught him to think so well, and consider what we might learn from their lessons.

We actually have very little information specific to Albert's early education. Based on general knowledge of his time and place, we know that formal education then was not universal but common only for those nobly born. We have seen that Albert was so blessed. Early formal education was usually received either at home or in a formal school setting, through teachers associated with the local cathedral or the local monastery.

The 19th-century biographer Sighart has argued that we can deduce further information about Albert's early education by our knowledge of the typical educational methods of the Benedictines, particularly those laid out in an educational treatise of the late 12th century, around the time of Albert's birth. It is to this medieval educational system that Sayers refers when she describes the "tools of learning": the tools that equip students to think and judge for themselves.

So what were the tools with which young Albert was equipped and could they be of any use to us today? The great medieval system of education was based on the seven "liberal arts." These were composed of the *trivium* (from *tri*, meaning "three," and *via*, meaning "roads" or "ways") of grammar, dialectics or logic, and rhetoric, and of the *quadrivium* (four ways) of music theory, astronomy, geometry, and mathematics. It is the *trivium* that Sayers, Albert's medieval teachers, and classical Greek and Roman educators saw as the fundamental tools for thinking, preparing one for adult life, and setting the stage for all future specialized knowledge.

Grammar came first, and Sighart notes this typically began at age seven.[7] For Albert this meant learning to read and write in Latin, the language of academia and of the Church (the very institution that made academia possible in that time). Books were quite rare, and the students would typically be read excerpts from the classical Roman grammarians such as Donatus, Prician, and Didymus. The teachers provided exposure to frequent repetition, and the students would be expected to memorize vocabulary words and grammatical rules. Explanations of the texts were also provided. Then came exposure to the Psalter, "whose chaunts he was made to learn by heart."[8] Indeed, Sighart opines that the psalms became as familiar to Albert as the "Our Father," as was evidenced by how frequently he incorporated them into his later writings. Further, Sighart offers, "It is only what man commits to memory from his tenderest years that can be preserved so faithfully and with such clearness in the sanctuary of his soul."[9]

From ages 9 to 11, Albert would have learned Aesop's fables, the poetry of Theodulus (a tenth-century writer whose verses were based on stories from the Old Testament), and also the sentences of the ancient Romans Cato the Moralist and Seneca the Stoic. Seneca was most prolific, and though a pagan, he provided much wisdom in full accord with Christian Truth. One of his moral recommendations, which might have impressed a young Albert, is this: "We need to set our affections on some good man and keep him constantly before our eyes, so that we may live as if he were watching us and do everything as if he saw what we were doing."[10] Other Latin writers studied at this time included Ovid, Horace, and the epic poet Virgil.

Then, after years of immersion in *grammar* and the ancient classical texts, students would become immersed in the study of *logic*—how to think and reason—and of *rhetoric*: the ability to write and speak effectively. Logical and rhetorical studies emphasized the writings of Marcus Tullius Cicero, Quintilian, and the great Greek philosopher Aristotle (in Latin translations, for Albert's studies did not include the Greek language). Teachers would urge Albert and other students not only to read these authors but also to meditate deeply on their words and, as much as possible, learn them by heart.

These early studies would serve Albert quite well throughout his life. His later scientific, philosophical, and even theological writings abound in citations of the great pagan thinkers, most especially Cicero, whom Albert would refer to familiarly as "Tully," and Aristotle, "the Philosopher." Albert later wrote in his book *The Sacrifice of the Mass* that although God revealed Himself to the Jewish people, "the sublimest wisdom the world could boast of flourished in Greece" because they "knew Him by the natural wisdom of reason."[11] He noted that the Greeks deduced just laws through reason alone and were favored by God to be the first Gentiles to receive the law of Christ. Albert thus set the tone for an entire school of Christian thought: Sighart asserts that a trademark of the medieval scholastic scholars was to seek Truth wherever it may be found.

Such was the salutary role of the *trivium* in Albert's early education. Today, proponents of "classical education" argue, like Sayers, that much can be gained by also teaching young modern students those three fundamental "ways." They say, for instance, that learning the grammar of an inflected language like Latin is a key to understanding and mastering one's own language and any other foreign tongue. Logic, which some modern educators have denigrated, claiming it produces no new knowledge, still provides the very useful function of sorting the true from the false, the valid from the invalid. Rhetoric, too, can afford a myriad of benefits. Sayers mentions how often we hear modern debaters, bereft of formal rhetorical training, talking past each other, failing to address each other's points or to define their own terms. The ancients took rhetoric very seriously, dividing it into five parts—invention, disposition, delivery, memory, and style—each involving an art and science of its own. Indeed, it was from the ancient rhetorical treatise attributed to Cicero, the *Ad Herennium*,[12] that Albert produced the rigorous analysis and improvement of the ancient art of memorization we will address in Chapter 5.

We can be certain that Albert found the *trivium* anything but trivial, because he chose to study the liberal arts with advanced education in the *trivium* and the *quadrivium* at the University of Padua. In the early 13th century, Europe boasted three great centers of advanced learning: the University of Paris led the world in the field of theology, Bologna led in canon and civic law, and Padua set the mark for the study of the liberal arts. When Albert was ready for his secondary education, around the year 1220, he crossed the Alps and walked the 350 miles to Padua in northeastern Italy, where he would further his education in those broad, liberal arts of learning.

ALBERT'S CRYSTAL-CLEAR INTELLIGENCE

Here is one of those cases where a report of questionable veracity about Albert's *life* nonetheless presents to us a truly valuable *lesson*. Some later biographers[13] (hence the questionable veracity) report that Albert's road to learning was not always a straight and easy path. In fact, they report that the Virgin Mary herself came to assist him in his studies, promising, as we saw in the quotation that begins this chapter, "that no one should surpass or equal him in learning."

The story goes that while in Padua, Albert became very frustrated in his attempts to learn science. Whatever he learned in the evening seemed to vanish from his mind by the time he arose in the morning. One day, when he was contemplating packing his bags and heading back to Germany, his room was brightly illuminated and there before him appeared three most beautiful virgins—Saints Barbara and Catherine, and the Blessed Virgin Mary, who asked Albert what he was seeking. Albert asked for vast knowledge of human wisdom. The Holy Virgin consented to give him philosophical knowledge without equal and also to protect him from being led away from his faith by this human knowledge. She also made it known that at the time before the end of his life this knowledge would be removed from him, and he would die as simple and innocent as a child.

Sighart says that such stories of Albert's difficulties in learning might have arisen from the sheer length of his studies in Padua. He notes that St. Dominic, who had much less interest in human science and wisdom, studied philosophy for six years, whereas Albert may have spent as many as ten. This may have given the suggestion to some that "the great one" was a little "slow," but it may really reflect more on his thoroughness.

Still, sometimes it is the slow and steady who win the race, and maybe even Albert had to work at it sometimes! As one biographer so eloquently puts it, "Science appeared to him very difficult at the commencement, and the path which led to it too thorny for his delicate feet; but, aided by an indefatigable application, he surmounted every obstacle. The marble receives with difficulty the form of a statue but retains it so much the better once the artist's chisel has imparted it to it: such was Albert's intelligence."[14] To the modern psychologist (to this one anyway), this calls to mind a modern distinction between "fluid" and "crystallized" forms of human intelligence. Though these concepts are nuanced, to put them in a nutshell, "fluid" intelligence refers to a mental quickness and facility to *learn* new things, while "crystallized" intelligence is the ability to *use* the skills, knowledge, and experience one has acquired over time.

We've all known people who seem to learn things without effort, who sail through school with a minimal investment of study, whereas others earn their knowledge and achieve their grades by the sweat of their brows. Some quick learners with high levels of fluid intelligence never get around to building up much crystallized intelligence, however. Consider the brilliant young man who sails through early studies by means of his quickness of wit and ability to think on his feet yet who, despite his deft reasoning abilities, is unable to get into the college or graduate school of his choice because he never spent enough time building up his crystallized intelligence. It is as if he allowed the fluid of his fluid intelligence to drain down a hole in the ground rather than flowing out into the things of the earth, encrusting them in its crystalline splendor.

So, if the lesson of the story holds true, it appears Albert built his great crystal cathedral of knowledge on the base of an ordinary fluid capacity. Albert's lesson for the modern student, then, is that the true test of your capacity to master learning is not whether its lessons come easy to you but whether you grasp them through diligent study and patient meditation.

OUTSIDE THE WALLS OF PADUAN ACADEME

Once the school day was over, many of Albert's peers donned silk coats, plumed hats, and bucklers and ventured out to enjoy the enjoy the sights and woo the ladies of their beautiful northern Italian setting. But Albert did not stray far from his future calling as scientist and saint. Even then he was more interested in the observation and explanation of natural phenomena.

Albert himself, in his *On Minerals*, tells of a time visiting Venice when he and a group of fellow students came across a block of marble—to be used in the construction of a church—that seemed to bear the perfect image of the head of a crowned king. Albert explained to his peers how the stone had been formed of "hardened vapors" and that excessive heat had caused them to rise to the center of the block in such a way that the image had been formed. He doesn't mention whether they then asked him why he couldn't just admire the canals like everybody else.

As for the saintly side of Albert, in those days he was also devout in his prayer, scriptural study, and Mass attendance. He especially liked to frequent Padua's Dominican church. In Chapter 6 we shall explore in more detail how St. Albert was drawn to the Order of Preachers and all that it entailed. Here, though, we'll progress right into Albert's next course of study, as the young man of burgeoning human wisdom turned the light of his intellect toward the wisdom of God.

SACRED SCIENCE STUDIES WITH THE SONS OF ST. DOMINIC

Biographers differ as to where the majority of Albert's training took place, some arguing that he stayed in Padua (though its university's theology program was not yet developed), some that he was sent to Paris, still others that he went to Cologne in his native Germany. It appears quite likely, though, that he spent a considerable amount of his novitiate 70 miles to the southwest of Padua, at the St. Nicholas Convent in Bologna. This is the convent where St. Dominic himself spent his last days, where his remains lay in repose at the time, and as Father Schwertner wrote so well, "the very corridors of the convent remained murmurous of his great zeal for souls, even as a shell reverberates the roar of the sea."[15]

Albert doesn't tell us exactly what he studied as a novice, and a standard program for Dominican formation had not yet been established (we'll see in the next chapter that Albert himself would be one of the men to establish it). Early biographers merely note that he devoted himself to study with a holy zeal and grew in manly virtue throughout this time. Still, we can deduce the general outline of his studies from our knowledge of the typical course of theological studies of his era.

Sighart notes Albert likely spent at least six years in his theological studies. Typically in the Middle Ages, theology students passed their first years of study as *Biblicii*—students of the Bible alone. Albert's consummate mastery of scripture shines through in all of his later theological writings. Next, students became *Sentenarii*—students of the *Sentences* of Peter Lombard (ca. 1100–1160), the preeminent systematic theologian of the previous century who heavily influenced both St. Albert and St. Thomas Aquinas. Albert also imbibed in great draughts the wisdom of the early Church Fathers and Doctors, for within their writings lived the foundational interpretations of scripture and the dogmas and doctrines on which Christ's Church is built.

Even during these years of Albert's twenties, stories or legends arose suggesting that his path to learning still was not an easy one. Some interject to this time period the story of the apparition of Mary we addressed earlier in this chapter. Perhaps the germ of this legend comes from a passage attributed to Albert in which he noted that he always felt inspired to study by the Holy Virgin and that what he could not master by study, he mastered through prayer. In any case, here again we see Albert as the model student who gains through noble effort and humble submission what might come more easily to others.

Many throughout the centuries have observed that perhaps the best way to truly master any body of knowledge is to learn it well enough to teach someone else. Well, part of the reason Albert was great, even in his day, was that he had so mastered many bodies of knowledge that he became the greatest *teacher* of his age and a great model for all times. So, after a look at the virtue of his studiousness, it makes sense to see what happened when the studious student became the talented teacher.

Great Idea #2: The Virtue of Studiousness

In the section on temperance in the *Summa Theologica*,[16] Albert's most studious student, St. Thomas Aquinas, carefully examines the virtue of *studiousness* and its opposing vice of *curiosity*. Both great saints acknowledge the veracity of Aristotle's statement that "all men desire to know"; the job of the virtue of studiousness is to temper or moderate that desire so that we seek to know the right things, at the right time, in the right manner, and for the right reasons.

In Albert's time, there was concern among some that the very study of nature and science would itself lead to the vice of curiosity (which derives from the Latin word *cura* for "care"—meaning, in this case, excessive care for the things of the world). Though it might sound strange to us, this concern is not baseless: in our day some of the most outspoken and ungracious champions of atheism are natural scientists, boldly daring to go beyond their own areas of expertise as they proclaim from their zealous faith in materialism that what we see is all we get.

The virtue of studiousness is an important thing for believers. As St. Thomas tells us, it is written in Proverbs 27:11, "Study wisdom, my son, and make my heart joyful."[17] The modern wonders of technology and the new media can spread the gospel and provide for spiritual instruction, communication, and inspiration in ways unfathomed by even such a prescient genius as St. Albert. But in today's technological age, the lures of curiosity also beckon as never before. My wife just bought me an egg timer to set beside my computer monitor so that the time I spend surfing the Web does not detract from my pursuit of spiritual wisdom—with book, not keyboard, in hand.

Chapter 3

Talented Teacher

A characteristic of one possessing Science is his ability
to teach.

—St. Thomas Aquinas[1]

At Paris Albert the Great himself lectured publicly and
with such marked success that the largest hall could not
hold his audiences.

—Hieronymous M. Wilson, O.P.[2]

I INVITE you to think back to your favorite teacher. (Although I'll
use the standard masculine pronouns, as one who received his
grade school education from dedicated Dominican nuns, I am well
aware that your favorite might well be a woman.) All right then, why
was he your favorite? What was he like? What did he say or do that
set him apart? In what ways did you (or do you still) aspire to be like
him?

My favorite high school teacher was a veritable 20th-century
St. Albert: a brilliant Viatorian priest who taught the highest level
science and mathematics courses and who, though he'd once been
recruited by NASA, chose instead to spend his life shaping unruly
and pimply teens into men of intelligence and character. What stands
out in my recollection about this great teacher is not only his towering
intelligence but also his intellectual discipline, his studiousness, and
his drive for total mastery of his subject matter. I remember him mat-
ter-of-factly stating that whenever he took a science or mathematics

course, he would make sure he worked out and understood every single problem, exercise, test question, and example in the book! (Father Pisors's great learning was won by the sweat of his brow, as was Albert's before him.)

Father also expected disciplined self-control in his students. Tardiness was a serious business. He handed back our tests in the order of their scores, from the highest to the lowest, for all our peers to see! And yet, though unyielding and all-knowing as an Aristotle in front of the class, when speaking to you one-on-one he revealed a glowing personal warmth.

Another favorite, my mentor in neuropsychology, shared the same zeal for total mastery of his subject matter, and though less structured, restrained, and self-disciplined, Dr. Zec exuded matchless passion, enthusiasm, and joy in learning.

Did *your* favorite teacher share any of these traits? Did he demonstrate true mastery and joy in learning? Did he show a personal concern for you and a desire to instill in you a wonder for learning and the self-discipline to pursue it to your greatest capacity? Did he challenge you because he wanted to see you grow?

St. Albert was among the very greatest teachers of his century or of any century, so surely he had such traits in abundance. Let's look know at what we can unearth from the depths of history to learn just what this great teacher was like, what he taught, how he taught it, and why we should all aspire to follow in his formidable footsteps.

PROVINCIAL PROFESSOR

We have no documents that specify the time or location of Albert's ordination into the priesthood, but recent scholars conjecture that this would have been some time shortly after the end of his theological studies, in approximately the year 1233. Albert was assigned right off the bat to the title of *lector* at the Dominican convent in Cologne, roughly 300 miles to the east of Paris, where he would later be sent to obtain his doctorate, and roughly 300 miles to the northwest of

Ratisbon (known today as Regensburg), where he would later carry his bishop's staff.

Now, *lector* is Latin for "reader," and we'll examine in a bit Albert's rapid ascent from "reader" to learned "doctor"—the first from Germany. But Albert's biographers are quick to note that he was not merely an academic master; no, the great Dominican was also a *pedagogue* in the most classical and highest sense of the word. Deriving from the Greek words παιδ (*paid*) for "boys," and αγογοσ (*agogos*) for "teacher," the true pedagogue did not merely teach academic subject matters, he trained and led young men to grow in wisdom and virtue as well. Perhaps when you think back to your own favorite teacher, you also have a true pedagogue in mind?

Though burgeoning new universities were forming in great cities such as the aforementioned Paris, Bologna, and Padua, the state of formal and higher education in Europe was really rather abysmal during the days of Albert's youth. Those turbulent times produced far more warriors and farmers than professors and scholars, and the great shepherds of the Church were well aware of the problem. The newly founded Order of Preachers had a rule that each of its convents would run a school, obligatory for all the brethren and even the prior, and open to the general public. That's one reason many bishops jumped at the chance to welcome communities of Dominicans to their dioceses, and some even studied there themselves.

Albert was first assigned teaching duties at the convent in Cologne. What might it have been like to sit at the feet of this great master in the full flower of his youth? Unless I'm mistaken, I do believe St. Thomas speculated that the resurrected body might well be that of a 33-year-old, before our powers start to decline. Imagine then young Albert, freshly ordained and burning to share the fruits of his studies of creation and Creator. There he stands, broad of shoulder and clear of gaze, in pristine white Dominican garb, communicating the depths of his understanding of Aristotle's matchless *logic*, his noble *ethics*, and his earthly wise *physics*. Hear him as he makes the scriptures come alive and complements the *Sentences* of Peter Lombard with eloquent sentences of his own.

Lector Albert's success as a teacher is attested to by his frequent assignments to establish new chapter schools throughout the German Dominican province. When Bishop Conrad II invited the Dominicans to his episcopal seat of Hildesheim in 1233, Albert was his superior's choice for apostolic pedagogue and organizer of the school. Despite this honor, in keeping with the character of our great scientist, the only recorded fact about this period of his life is his reference to seeing a comet that was documented as far away as China.

The next stop was the Bavarian town of Freiburg in the year 1235. Here again, he founded a school and was soon called elsewhere, leaving legends behind.[3] On Albert went, sharing of the fruits of his contemplation with his brethren in Strasburg, where Dominicans had settled in 1223, commissioned to open a school of theology. Not all were pleased, though, with the friars' arrival. Some local professors of the city were disgruntled to find their own students leaving their schools for those of the sons of St. Dominic. Still, the city honored St. Albert with a statue on its cathedral's famous astronomical clock.

Next we find Albert for two years in Ratisbon, teaching in a diocese that he would head as its bishop in middle age. The city had been blessed by the Hohenstein emperors with a bounty of beautiful schools and churches, and Dominicans had been present there since 1218. Albert taught Aristotelian philosophy, grammar, mathematics, astronomy, and metaphysics, his broad genius and peerless grasp of the secrets of nature already giving rise to whispers that he must possess magical powers.

Albert's esteem among his brethren was growing, as demonstrated by his election as delegate to two provincial chapter meetings during this time. In 1238 in Bologna, he was among the frontrunners to succeed Blessed Jordan of Saxony as master general of the entire order, but he withdrew his name from the ballot. Though the details are not known, we can observe that though Albert would go on to wear many hats, including the bishop's miter; those hats were bestowed upon him, and he accepted them in accord with his vows of obedience to his order and to the pope. Albert himself seemed to cherish most, and deem most fitting for himself, the doctor's cap of a teaching master. It is to that role that he returned time and again of his own volition when he was not obliged by his superiors to take on other duties.

DOMINICAN DOCTOR, PRIDE OF PARIS

As is the case for many (though by no means all) of the key events in Albert's life, accounts are incomplete and estimates vary as to exact dates and durations. Nonetheless, we can be confident that somewhere between the mid-1230s and 1240, Albert was sent to the University of Paris to attain the great honor of being the first German to wear the doctor's cap in theology. So off he started—being a good Dominican, on foot—on this journey of several hundred miles.

When Albert arrived at the "island in the Seine"[4] its population was estimated to be about 100,000 in the city proper and about 120,000 including surrounding areas, immense for the time, but a far cry from the approximately 12 million living in the metropolitan area of Paris today. (That's a hundred-fold increase, yet is there even one more St. Albert among all of today's Parisians?) So Albert arrived in France, the Bible in one hand, Aristotle and Lombard in the other. We know that Aristotle and Lombard were Albert's "masters" in a sense, and he mastered their writings like no one before him. Still, unlike the young St. Thomas Aquinas, we know very little about Albert's own teaching masters as he worked diligently and swiftly toward his doctorate.

Weisheipl has discerned, however, that in 1245 Albert incepted in theology under a Gueric of Saint-Quentin, the second Dominican to hold the Dominican chair "for foreigners" outside of France. Little is known of Gueric's personality or teaching style, though we do have written record of nine of his "qudolibets" or "disputed questions" from around the year 1240. These were standard academic exercises in which students would pose formal questions on things philosophical and theological, to be answered in depth by the master. Each "question" was actually composed of many smaller questions, addressing such issues as Church history and liturgy, the nature of the body and soul, moral theology, the nature of angels and demons, and much more, even in the small sample we have of master Gueric's work.

From Gueric's long tenure as Dominican chair in the premier university theology department in the world, we can deduce great competence and dedication (Albert himself would be inspired to fill his vacated chair for three years from 1245 to 1248, and in 1256 St. Thomas Aquinas sat in that same chair for a three-year stint of his own). Paris was considered the center of "new learning," the latest and greatest of Christian thought, and the most cherished spot for world-class philosophers and theologians. Whatever the other characteristics of Albert's academic masters, it seems we can be confident that their theological knowledge was of the very highest caliber.

Another thing we know is that for two very good reasons, 1244 was a most momentous year for Albert of Cologne in Paris. That year, he became a doctor of theology, the pride of the Dominicans and the first from all of Germany. It was also in that year that Albert began to experience the greatest joy and fulfillment of a true pedagogue, a joy that would endure for the next three decades. To quote an unlikely source (19th-century American poet Walt Whitman) for a parallel,

I am the teacher of athletes,
He that by me spreads a wider breast than my own proves the
    width of my own,
He most honors my style who learns under it to destroy the
    teacher.[5]

St. Albert would encounter that year at Paris a young intellectual and spiritual athlete with an unquenchable hunger for his training and an unequalled capacity to digest and absorb it. Like the ancient unconquerable Olympic wrestler Milo, who could pin any opponent with the power he'd built from lifting a bull, this young "ox" of southern Italy could not be bested in logical disputation. Still, he would never pin, let alone "destroy," his teacher; rather, the two would train and inspire each other to ever greater feats of intellectual and spiritual strength throughout their days on Earth.

St. Albert is certainly best known as the teacher of St. Thomas Aquinas. Surely our great saint is pleased by this, and we will examine their relationship more fully toward the end of our story, but for now I'll simply recount their most famous early incident, and one lesser known exchange.

The Dominican novice Thomas of Aquino, Albert's junior by about 25 years, was only barely out of his teens when he came to Paris to study with Albert. Judged by his massive size and his quiet demeanor, he was presumed by his worldly wise peers to be a bit of an oaf and perhaps a country bumpkin. One of those peers was in for an eye-opener when he presumed to "help" St. Thomas with a difficult lesson, only to have the normally taciturn Thomas proceed to explain the passage to him with a depth of understanding that made his would-be tutor's jaw drop. Albert himself had come across a crumpled note of Thomas's commentary on a difficult passage from St. Dennis[6] and was astounded at his perspicacity. He assigned young Thomas the task of handling a difficult topic in public disputation the next day—some even conjecture that his disputant would be Albert himself. Here is how Sighart characterizes their interchange after Thomas had had his say:

> "Brother Thomas . . . you appear to perform less the part of respondent than that of master . . . The conclusions come within the master's province, and you speak as though you were already a master."
>
> "Master," Thomas modestly replied, "I know not how to treat the question otherwise."[7]

Albert knew that his peers had dubbed young Thomas "the dumb ox of Sicily," and Albert famously informed them that the bellowing of this ox would be heard around the world. Indeed, it echoes to this very day.

Methods of the Medieval Master

The University of Paris, incorporated by the year 1200, produced the cream of the theological crop of the Middle Ages. Not only could it boast of the likes of Sts. Albert and Thomas and the Franciscan St. Bonaventure, but it would produce nine future popes. We are told how Albert's masterful teaching drew in vast audiences, including the rich and the poor, young and old, prelates and princes, religious and secular from far and wide over Europe. Of Albert's great influence there we can still see the signs today—such as street signs indicating the *Rue Maitre Albert* (Master Albert Street) and the *Place Maubert* (*Maubert* was reportedly a contraction of the French for "Master Albert"), just moments' walk from the Cathedral of Notre Dame. So what were the methods by which St. Albert helped produce such learned and saintly souls and made such a deep impression on one of the world's great cities?

By the time Albert reached Paris, all stories of his difficult path to learning had ceased. He quickly rose from the ranks of the bachelor, who sat on a lower bench and taught simpler subjects, to that of high-seated master. Later, Doctor Albert would serve in one of the two Dominican chairs at the university at that time.

Albert was then already known for his encyclopedic knowledge of things natural and supernatural and for his saintly patience in fielding the questions of his students. Still, though the picture of longanimity in bearing with the struggles of his students, he held high his expectations for them. He was a stickler for detailed note-taking and for extensive memorization. Students were required to participate in discussions and review of all their lessons once each week, to participate in disputations—in which the lector or junior professor would object to and argue against the students' theses—once each month, and to argue against theses defended by their professors in disputations open to the public twice each year. (Surely this is more than enough to shiver the timbers of the coddled modern college student!)

Even taking notes was a privileged enterprise, since writing materials, like books, were preciously scarce. (Recall that Gutenberg's printing press still lay two centuries in the future.) And with total mastery of material the goal for professors and students, memory was of the utmost importance. Schwertner invites us to imagine the students after their classroom sessions straining to memorize: seated on long wooden benches or bundles of straw, repeating their notes on the road to and from school, using "mental gymnastics, in the form of jingling verses."[8] Yet as we shall see in Chapter 5, if these were Albert's students, they may well have had access to some very special "mental gymnastics" for memorization, going far beyond jingles, and culled from the ancients by none other than Albert himself.

At the Feet of the Universal Doctor

Can you imagine what it would have been like to sit in Master Albert's classroom, listening to the great man at the height of his powers shedding new light on the mysteries of creation and the Creator? What teaching traits and talents would he have demonstrated? Words that come to my mind, in addition to things like the *diligence, discipline, intellect,* and *memory for facts* of the learned scientist include the *passion, enthusiasm, wonder, awe, gratitude, knowledge base, interconnectivity, creativity,* and *inspiration* of the true pedagogue.

Aristotle began his book *Metaphysics* with the simple line, "All men by their natures desire to know." He elaborated that we see this "by the delight that they take in their senses." This is where *passion* comes into play. We are mind-body unities. Our bodily senses and our spirit operating through them are *passive* or *passable*—receptive, movable by the goods of creation that become known to us through our senses. Through our natural passions, we are hard-wired by God to seek out the good, though it is through our trained *reason* that we build the capacity to seek out which good things are truly the best for us! Through passions we also combat evils that keep us from the good. We saw in the first chapter a graphic example of the great

scientist's passion for worldly learning in his chiding of the preachers and "ignorant people" within his own order, who like "animals"
would denigrate such sensible knowledge.

Enthusiasm derives from the Greek *enthusiazien*, "to be inspired
by a god." Albert, of course, was inspired not by *a* god, but by *the*
God. We will see in the next chapter that Albert knew well how
natural virtues build on our human natures—our passions, intellect,
and will—and that *natural* virtues are perfected when our actions
are guided by right reason. *Supernatural* virtues and gifts, however,
are infused in us from God. They perfect our actions, not merely in
accord with our human reason, but in accord with the promptings and
stirrings of the Holy Spirit within our souls. Surely it was obvious,
to the thousands of young students and veteran scholars of Europe
pouring into Albert's overflowing classrooms, that here was no man
to sing to cold reason a hymn. No man could be as "fired up" as
was Albert to teach about so many subjects, natural and divine, for
so many years, in so many settings, with so much success, despite
so many other diversions and responsibilities, unless his heart was
inflamed by the Holy Spirit. I have no doubt that his students could
see it on his face.

Wonder, awe, and *gratitude* abound in the writings of Albert and
of those who wrote about him. This same man who refined Aristotle's theories of metaphysics, causation, astronomy, and physiology,
who wrote learned treatises on the Holy Eucharist and on the types
and divine graces of the Virgin Mary, records with great care and joy
the habits of the squirrel and the defining characteristics of the flowers in the local woods. Surely, Albert's students saw a teacher who
conveyed the understanding that whatever subjects they studied, no
matter how obviously lofty or apparently trivial, spoke of the bounteous generosity of a good and loving God who provided us a world
with wonders great and small. (How sad is the contrast that so many
of today's students of the sciences are taught by teachers who think of
the universe as the purposeless result of blind chance? Where is the
wonder and awe and to whom can they pay gratitude?)

In her *Book of Memory*, Modern English professor Mary Carruthers provides an interesting comparison and contrast between the characteristics of Albert Einstein and St. Thomas Aquinas, citing the writings of men who knew them well. She notes that the trait most often cited in Einstein was that of his awesome *creativity*, whereas for St. Thomas it was his prodigious *memory*. Thomas, it was said, remembered virtually everything he read. His mind was like a laser beam, focused with incredible intensity on philosophical and theological writings and burning them into the deep and spacious recesses of his saintly memory.

Perhaps even a more fruitful and direct comparison would be between the two Alberts, both the greatest scientists of their day. If *creativity* is among Einstein's crowning intellectual glories, and *memory* among Thomas's, I would suggest that *an incredibly broad knowledge base* is the foundation from which Albert's singular greatness as a teacher was built.

Thomas's mind was that awesome, focused laser beam, unparalleled in depth of penetration. Albert's mind was a broad and powerful searchlight, unparalleled in the breadth and illumination of its rays, sweeping and searching the earth and the heavens, shedding light on whatever hints of wisdom and reflections of God's glory that fell within its path. Over years of diligent study, Albert had acquired an encyclopedic knowledge of things earthly and divine. He was the man who knew everything there was to know.

We learn new, unfamiliar things in the light of old, familiar things we already know well. Albert's huge base of knowledge therefore allowed for an incredible awareness of the "*inconnectivity*" or relatedness of things. One aspect of creativity has been described as the ability to perceive hidden likenesses or similarities. When a student has an "Aha!" experience of understanding, a sense of "Now I get it!" chances are he has seen how this new piece of knowledge, this fact or this insight, fits or makes sense in the context of things that he already knows. With Albert's unsurpassed base of knowledge and awareness of the interrelatedness of things, certainly students who paid careful heed to this master's lessons would have abounded in "Ahas!" every day. Can't you just imagine their looks of surprise and delight, and hear their satisfied murmurings echoing throughout the halls of the University of Paris and of so many Dominican houses of study?

The last of the characteristics of Albert as teacher that I'll speculate on here is that of *inspiration*. Communicating his own innate sense of wonder about the universe, Albert both inspired his students along the same lines and left them open to the supernatural inspiration of the Holy Spirit. We saw earlier the brief testimony from Ulric of Strasbourg about his teacher's greatness. One classroom observer remarked how one student "had no sooner heard [Master Albert] expound every science with such wondrous depth of wisdom, than he rejoiced exceedingly at having so quickly found that which he had come to seek, one who offered him so unsparingly the fulfillment of his heart's desire."[9] These are the words of William of Tocco, reporting on the reaction of young St. Thomas Aquinas.

Albert taught and wrote at Paris until the summer of 1248, when he was called back by his brothers to become regent of a new *Studium Generale*, a house of advanced studies for the Dominicans in Cologne, where his genius, as well as his sanctity, and the "force of his doctrine" drew students and scholars from around the world.[10] And St. Thomas was among those who journeyed with St. Albert to further build and disperse the "new learning" of Paris among their brother friars in Cologne. Two years later, we find Albert at Valenciennes in northern France, helping draft the official system of study for the Order of Preachers.

As we shall see throughout this book, over his life Albert was often on the move in this way, going from one great work to the next. Let us follow his example and switch gears ourselves, moving from the classroom to the study, from the orator to the thinker, from Albert teacher to Albert the philosopher.

GREAT IDEA #3: THE VIRTUE OF MAGNIFICENCE

As we shall see in the next chapter, in defining the essential "parts" of the virtue of fortitude, the Roman philosopher Cicero, St. Albert, and St. Thomas were all unanimous in including the virtue of *magnificence*. Note, if you will, its etymological resemblance to "magnanimity," or greatness of soul, another of the essential parts of fortitude. *Magnificence* derives from Latin words *magnus* for "great" and *facere* for "to do or to make." The magnificent man, then, is he who does or makes great things.

Traditional renderings of magnificence emphasized the expenditure of money in contributing to great causes or accomplishing great public works. A great man shows fortitude, fearlessness in the face of potential hardships, by his willingness to part with his money so that others might derive great good from it. We know that Albert came from a well-off family yet willingly embraced a vow of poverty to serve God and man within the Dominican order. In essence, he sold all that he had owned so that he could follow Him.[11] But there is another, broader, and very important sense in which Albert the Great was magnificent.

In his nearly lifelong recurring role as a teacher, St. Albert helped "build" saintly and learned *men* (and as we'll see in later chapters, plenty of saintly women, too). Besides Ulric and St. Thomas, Albert "bred a large offspring of eminent professors,"[12] including among many others, Blessed Ambrose Sansedonius, a champion of social justice and scourge of usurers and predatory bankers at the peril of his own safety; Francigenus, the prolific Dominican academic; and Denis of Viterbo, a powerful preacher *sans pareil* in his native province of Italy.

Chapter 4

Foundational Philosopher

Each thing's cause is either internal or external. If it is external, then it is either the "cause by which," and this is the efficient cause, or it is the "cause for the sake of which" and this is the final cause. If it is internal, either it is act, and this is the form, or it is potency, and this is matter.

—St. Albert the Great[1]

Albert is not merely an eclectic thinker, a recorder of opinions, and a proselytizer of Aristotelian doctrine, but rather a profoundly original theorist who wove together the data of classical and Aristotelian ethical theory into a strikingly original moral synthesis with evident neo-Platonic overtones.

—Stanley B. Cunningham[2]

WHEN our boys were little they loved this movie called *Robot Wars*. (Maybe they got their tastes from me, since my childhood favorites included such classics as *War of the Gargantuas* and *King Kong Escapes*.) It's set, as best as I can recall, in the world of the future after some cataclysmic war. Much of the world is a dangerous, barbarous wasteland. Tourists who venture to visit old 20th-century cities (now ghost towns) are conveyed in a giant robot shaped like a scorpion. This laser-loaded bus of sorts would protect tourists from marauders on their trips out into the vast wilderness. Well, it turned out that the company (or maybe it was the government—it's been awhile) that provided the giant scorpion was also in cahoots with the marauders and was really running the whole show.

A young guy and young gal uncover this state of affairs and in one of these ghost towns discover, hidden deep underground, an old yet massively powerful giant robot, shaped in the form of a man. They bring the colossus back to life, it defeats the scorpion, and the world is free again. Or something like that. Anyway, though the film never won critical acclaim, the boys gave it four thumbs up!

And what have giant robots to do with our foundational philosopher? Good question. In the early 13th century, European Christendom faced a powerful military menace from the deserts of the east, with the sting of the Saracen scimitar felt from Spain to the Holy Land. The Church was also faced with *intellectual* threats from the east and from within. Constantinople and the Christian Byzantine Empire trembled before the might of Islam. Old philosophies retrieved from the Greeks were being interpreted by some Muslim and even Christian philosophers such as Averroes and Peter Abelard to promote dangerous ideas that diminished the dignity and responsibility of individual men as persons, questioned the immortality of the soul, and blurred the essential difference between man and the other animals.

Enter Albert, the great philosophical warrior, who unearthed his own hidden war machine: a sleeping giant in the shape of a man. It was Albert who revived "the Philosopher," Aristotle of Stagira (384–322 BC) in his full, original splendor, casting the brilliant light of his intellect on the existence of God and the nature of man.

In the time of Albert's youth, Aristotle's works were little known in the Christian world, though Christianity—largely through the wisdom of St. Augustine and some others—had gained much from the philosophical insights of Aristotle's great teacher, Plato. Though Boethius had begun work on translating Aristotle into Latin and explaining his works in the early sixth century, Aristotle was known in the West only for a small selection of his works, primarily those on logic. Arab and Jewish philosophers had begun to comment on and interpret the whole body of Aristotle's works, but of course they looked at him through their own theological lenses, and they were working from relatively corrupt translations of the Stagirite's original works in Greek.

Some of the Christians who had heard of Aristotle considered him a threat to the Faith. It didn't help that his writings were relished (in their corrupted form) in the court of Emperor Frederick II, who by that time had been excommunicated and become an enemy of the Church.

Such was the perceived threat from Aristotle (the Aristotle known through corrupted translations and distorted commentaries) that in 1210 the Council of Sens in Paris determined that excommunication would be the lot of those who wrote commentaries on the books of Aristotle (though they could still be referred to in citations). In 1228 even the Dominican constitution forbade study of the works of pagan philosophers. Fortunately, in 1231, Pope Gregory IX allowed for the prohibition to be lifted when the translations were corrected.

A few decades later, Dominican scholar William of Moeberke, purportedly at the request of Thomas Aquinas, would answer the call and translate the works of the Stagirite directly from the oldest and least corrupted original Greek texts. Both Sts. Albert and Thomas would avail themselves aplenty of these works and write many line-by-line commentaries of many of them. And indeed they showed that the learned master of reason's views of man, of the universe, and of God were no threat to Christianity but rather helped form an impregnable barrier to many errors, forming the foundation of a *philosphia perennis*: a philosophy of basic truths holding good for all times.

MASTERING MEDIEVAL METAPHYSICS

Of Albert's scientific bent, and his interest in the things of the natural world, there is no doubt. Yet in his own day he was referred to as a *magnus philosophus*, and even as the *maximus in philosophia*[3] even before he achieved fame as a scientist. Science looks at causes and effects in the natural world; it looks for relationships, for laws of nature, for explanations of how things work the way they do. But higher is the field of study that examines even science itself, a field that transcends or goes beyond physics, the field of *meta*physics.

Metaphysics examines not only natural things and phenomena and causes and effects and laws; it also questions why there even *are* things and events and causes and effects and laws. It seeks not only to find that A causes B and B causes C but to determine who or what got the whole alphabet of causation rolling in the first place—and why. Aristotle started his book *Metaphysics* with the line, "All men by nature desire to know."[4] Who in the 13th century more ardently desired knowledge, or achieved a broader base of it, than Albert himself? Aristotle also noted that it is better to know a little about sublime things than a great deal about petty things. Sublime things are the subject matter of metaphysics. Aristotle compares it to wisdom, indeed in its highest reaches to divine wisdom, for it seeks to discover through our reason what Aristotle called God.

Albert would thoroughly digest Aristotle's philosophical writings in metaphysics and more, writing invaluable commentaries in which he sought to paraphrase and make understandable Aristotle's own thought. He interjected relatively little of his own opinions in these commentaries, leaving it for his later works and for the work of his followers (especially St. Thomas) to build from Aristotle's base that aforementioned *philosophia perennis*.

Now, as with his scientific writings, some throughout history have criticized Albert for simply parroting Aristotle, but this isn't really fair. Albert wrote his commentaries primarily to counter corruptions and to make Aristotle known by his own true ideas. Further, as we will see in the sections that follow, Albert sometimes broke with Aristotle in elements of his philosophical psychology, staying closer to St. Augustine and sometimes attempting a synthesis of the two. In his ethics, we will see how Albert incorporated seminal Ciceronian and neo-Platonic perspectives. And indeed, can there be plainer evidence of the injustice of the charge than an entire section in Albert's own *Summa Theologica* titled "The Errors of Aristotle?"[5]

PHILOSOPHICAL PSYCHOLOGY

Ask an attentive modern student of psychology about the birth of psychology and you may well hear about Wilhelm Wundt's famous psychological laboratory, established at the University of Leipzig, Germany in 1879. Actually though, that marked merely the birth of modern *experimental* or *scientific psychology* as a distinct academic discipline. Psychology itself, by definition from the ancient Greek, being the formal study of the *psyche,* or mind, has been around as long as there have been human beings with minds inclined to ponder themselves.

Philosophical psychology seeks to examine the nature of man based on our interior experience and our public experience of each other's behavior. It has existed as an important discipline since the time of the ancient Greek philosophers, millennia before the establishment of any particular university laboratory. *Scientific psychology* can conduct controlled experiments and structured observational and correlational studies that flesh out the details and enhance our picture of how the mind works and how we behave, but the core of what we are—of what it means to possess the unique powers and capacities of the human soul—this is the stuff of the philosophical psychologist, and this field too can boast of a most influential German professor.

We've seen how deeply Albert cared about all of God's creatures, how he studied them with rapt concentration and joy. Well, the creature he loved the most and studied most deeply was man himself.

Albert found much wisdom in the *content* of Aristotle's portrayal of the human soul, especially in Aristotle's work *De Anima* (On the Soul), and in his books on related topics such as memory, sensation, dreams, and ethics. The Stagirite defines the soul as the form giving life to the body, as characterized by vegetative, sensitive, and rational levels, each with its own powers; he also examines what psychologists today are calling "information processing," that is, how information gleaned from the outside world moves through the faculties of our senses and into the higher reaches of our minds.

But Albert also found great wisdom in Aristotle's *basic approach to the subject* (an approach that also drew me in to the writings of Aristotle, Albert, and Thomas). Aristotle never presumed that all important thought began with him. No, he made it a point to carefully survey the ideas of great thinkers who came before him, only afterward to offer his own criticisms and arguments. Albert also made himself intimately familiar with the ideas of great thinkers and commentators, including Jewish and Muslim philosophers.

Albert, like Aristotle before him and St. Thomas after him, elaborated a detailed understanding of human nature, of the interconnections between body and soul. He denoted the layers or levels of the soul, from the powers of growth and reproduction, hallmarks of the *vegetative soul* of plants, to the powers of the senses and locomotion characterizing the *sensitive soul* of animals, to the powers of intellect and will, unique to human beings with our *rational souls*. He helped expound a detailed process whereby our human intellects come to know and understand abstract ideas and universal concepts.

When 20th-century psychology finally began to extricate itself from the decades of mindless musings by the behaviorist psychologists who downplayed or denied the role of the mind and the will, there began in the 1960s a "cognitive revolution" in academic psychology and in applied psychotherapy. Academics produced "information processing models" examining the steps and processes of how we learn, know, and remember. And clinicians elaborated systems of "cognitive therapy" that reflected how we could train ourselves to bring our emotions and behaviors in line with rational thinking. In making these philosophical "advances," they were merely retracing a great deal of ground traversed centuries ago by the patron saint of science.

For a couple of specific examples, take two highly successful systems of therapy founded in the 1950s and 1960s: psychologist Albert Ellis's rational-emotive therapy and psychiatrist Aaron Beck's cognitive therapy. Both men reacted to a Freudian overemphasis on human beings as the helpless pawns of unconscious drives and emotions. Both systems are based on the fundamental premise that we function best and are least prone to psychological disturbance when our emotions and actions derive from careful, rational thinking and realistic assessments of ourselves and the situations we encounter out in the world. Centuries before, St. Albert had meticulously detailed how in order to attain happiness, our passions must be guided by our intellectual powers of "right reason." He addressed these issues most explicitly in his writings on ethics and the virtues, and it is to this topic that we turn next.

ETHICS: ST. ALBERT ON THE GOOD LIFE

St. Albert wrote more than one treatise on moral behavior and ethics throughout his long and illustrious life. His most influential, titled *De Bono* (On the Good), was written at the height of his powers in the middle of his career. In answering the philosophical question of what is good for man (and thus how we should act), Albert knew that first he had to know man's *nature*. He knew that in order to know what we *ought* to do, we need to know what we *are*.

Albert was bold, courageous, and influential in the way that he synthesized classical pagan views on the nature of the soul and of virtue (virtue being in one sense the perfection of the powers of the soul) with the Christian anthropology taught by the Church Fathers—and most predominantly by St. Augustine, who himself built on Plato. That Augustinian-Platonic view of man's nature and his perfection placed tremendous relative emphasis on God's *special grace* and relatively little emphasis on man's God-given *nature*.

For example, in his theory of man's intellectual powers of understanding concepts and universal principles, St. Augustine described a supernatural process of *illumination* whereby to make a true judgment of things, man's mind must be directly acted upon by God. Aristotle, on the contrary, described a natural process of *abstraction* based on the receptivity of our sense organs and our intellects to the forms of things in the outside world. By the workings of our (God-given) intellectual powers, we *abstract*, or draw forth, the essences of things and arrive at natural truths without direct divine intervention. Albert attempted a theory that incorporated both processes.[6]

Albert accomplished something similar (later to be crowned, as his thought so often was, with the finishing touches of St. Thomas) in his approach to natural *virtues*. Again due to the profound influence of St. Augustine, most Catholic thinkers of the Middle Ages greatly downplayed the role and some even the *existence* of natural goodness and virtue. Recall how influential was the *Sentences* of Peter Lombard in theological education in Albert's time. Here is Lombard's definition of virtue: "a good quality of mind by which one lives aright, and which no one uses badly, which God alone effects in man."[7] So even things like the classic "cardinal" moral virtues that the wise pagans wrote about, namely temperance, fortitude, justice, and prudence, were seen to be perfections *infused in man directly by God* rather than developed through the use of man's natural powers.

Albert turned this view around. The great naturalist saw so well the inherent greatness of nature, in this instance, human nature. And yet, since God in his generosity gave us that nature, he knew that the natural virtues are by no means a repudiation of his causality. Unlike the ancient pagan sages, who had the benefit of neither revelation nor sanctifying grace, however, St. Albert also knew that only supernatural intervention from God can show the very highest truths and goods at which we should aim our efforts and allow us to attain them.

In his examination of natural virtue, Albert considered many definitions of virtue in addition to Peter Lombard's. The Roman Cicero, for example, defined virtue as "a habit of mind in harmony with reason and the order of nature,"[8] while Aristotle called virtue "a voluntary state of character lying in a mean, the mean relative to us, this being determined by reason and as the wise man will determine it."[9] Note here how natural virtue is a *habit*, something difficult that we train ourselves up to and build over time, that it flows from harmony with human *natural reason* rather than the direct illumination of God, and that it is voluntary, denoting a connection to the human will.

Finally, it is a *mean*, that is, a *state of excellence* or *balance* that is neither excessive nor deficient, neither too much nor too little.

By emphasizing these and other elements of natural virtue, St. Albert puts us in the best position to understand what these virtues are, which of our human powers they perfect, and how we might pursue them. Though I have not the space to consider the complex nature of these virtues as Albert lays them out for us, you will find many of them sketched out in the "Great Ideas" boxes within the pages of this book. For now, I'd like to give you just a taste of how Albert, in his book *De Bono*, wonderfully synthesized classical pagan virtue theory with divine revelation. In examining how virtues are means, Albert gave examples of how common sins are vices of excess or deficiency. In detailing how, in contrast, virtues perfect our human powers, he paved the way for an understanding of many related virtues and "parts" of the four great cardinal virtues, which parts could then be incorporated into a life of grace and holiness.

Albert, the master, and Thomas, his greatest student, both detailed the "parts" of the cardinal virtues, in similar though slightly different ways. Take a look at a couple of examples in the following table.

THE PARTS OF FORTITUDE		THE PARTS OF PRUDENCE	
St. Albert	**St. Thomas**	**St. Albert**	**St. Thomas**
Magnificence	Magnanimity	Memory	Memory
Confidence	Magnificence	Intelligence	Understanding
Patience	Patience	Foresight	Docility
Perseverance	Perseverance		Reason
			Shrewdness
			Foresight
			Circumspection
			Caution

So why the similarities and why the differences? The virtue of fortitude, for example, deriving from the Latin *fortis* for "strength," perfects our ability to undertake and sustain difficult tasks or hardships that would deprive us of some good. It puts our iras-cible passions, deriving from the Latin *ira* for "anger," under the guidance of our reason so that we may fight the good fight. The extreme Christian example of fortitude is martyrdom, the strength and endurance to confront even death if it stood between us and our highest good—God Himself. In its everyday garden variety, forti-tude comes into play any time we stand up for what is right, or do or endure hard things of any kind because we know it's the right thing to do. Of these basic attributes of fortitude, our two great saints are fully agreed.

Next we come to what they called the "integral parts," related virtues that give to fortitude its full force and strength. When Sts. Albert and Thomas wrote their monumental works on natural virtues, they borrowed freely from previous philosophers and from scripture and the Church Fathers. In the case of fortitude, Albert borrowed his four integral parts from Cicero, a man many considered "protoevan-gelical" in his philosophy. Cicero defined courage, a synonym of fortitude, as the "deliberated undertaking of dangerous tasks and the enduring of hardships."[10] He defined its four integral parts as mag-nificence or high-mindedness (*magnificentia*), confidence (*fidentia*), patience (*patientia*), and perseverance (*perseverantia*). These are the related virtues that aid us in thinking about and undertaking great tasks and sticking with them even when trials or delays occur.

St. Thomas too culled wisdom from wherever he found it in previous thinkers, and he chose three of Cicero's four parts of forti-tude, substituting magnanimity for confidence (which he classed as a related "annexed" virtue rather than as integral part). Magnanim-ity he drew from Aristotle's writings on human virtue, primarily from his *Nicomachean Ethics*, a book known inside and out by both our great saints (both wrote commentaries on its every line). Mag-nanimity, greatness of soul, was of course the crowning virtue of St. Albert himself.

Let's turn now for a moment to *prudence*. This is the practical wisdom that finds the best means for moral ends, the virtue that "gets the job done." In the complementarity of writings on prudence, Sts. Albert and Thomas ever so prudently got the job done, providing us with a wealth of practical wisdom we can put to use today.

Albert once again borrows from Cicero: in this case, his three integral parts of memory, intelligence, and foresight. These emphasize the aspects of prudence that build on the knowledge of the past to predict future outcomes in line with present actions. To Cicero's parts St. Thomas also incorporates the parts as well of the fourth-century Latin scholar Macrobius, arriving at his own full eight integral parts: memory, understanding or intelligence, docility, reason, shrewdness, foresight, circumspection, and caution. Albert was aware of Macrobius too, but in his scheme Albert considered the eight integral parts annexed or related virtues.

Now, I have a special interest in one of those parts, having written a book (*Memorize the Faith!*) on memory techniques based on the writings of St. Albert in *De Bono* and St. Thomas in his *Summa Theologica*. I emphasize St. Thomas's special contribution to the understanding and perfection of memory as a part of prudence in that book, and in the next chapter of *this* book, we'll examine St. Albert's special role in the understanding of human memory, both in how it works and in how to perfect it. But for now, let's take one last look at Albert, the *philosophus maximus*!

ALBERT'S GREAT BRIDGE FROM ATHENS TO ROME

St. Thomas Aquinas is usually credited with "baptizing" Aristotle and forming the bridge between his philosophy of *reason* and the *revelation* of the good news of Christ. Even unbelievers praise him for reintroducing Aristotle's thought to the Western world. It would be an exercise in understatement to describe as "monumental" St. Thomas's role in showing how Aristotle's philosophy (to the degree that it reflected the truth) was totally consistent with Christian revelation. And yet in truth, it was Albert, his master, who first built a "bridge" between Aristotle and Christ, between Athens and Rome.

St. Albert was also an extremely important philosopher in his own right for his contributions to our understanding of the very nature of the universe in his metaphysics to the nature of man in his philosophical psychology and the means of man's fulfillment through grace perfecting nature in his philosophy and theology of virtue ethics. He saw philosophy—as did Socrates, Plato, Aristotle, and the Stoics—not as some academic sport of linguistic and logical gymnastics but as a guide to the understanding and appreciation of the wonders of creation and the Creator and as a source of practical advice for living the kinds of lives on Earth that will bring both earthly happiness and eternal bliss.

GREAT IDEA #4: THE VIRTUE OF WISDOM

Who is wise and understanding among you? By his good
life let him show his works in the meekness of wisdom.

—James 3:13

We have seen that St. Albert was a consummate philosopher in the literal sense: "philosophy" is made up of *philos* (love) of *sophia* (wisdom). Albert sought not merely a passing worldly wisdom but the eternal wisdom that derives from God. St. James tells us that "if any of you lacks wisdom, let him ask God";[11] Albert asked God for wisdom and kept asking every day of his life for both the theoretical wisdom of the highest truths and the practical wisdom of prudence that is applied in the simple acts of our daily lives.

James also tells us that "the wisdom from above is first pure, then peaceable, gentle, open to reason, fully of mercy and good fruits, without uncertainty or insincerity."[12] From his Dominican vow of chastity to his official duties as a peacemaker to the many and bounteous fruits of his contemplation, Albert loved and embodied wisdom like few others before or since.

In his own writings, Albert endorsed the practice of the wisdom that comes from the careful, reasoned reflection on the nature and workings of creation, but he held that the higher wisdom is that which elicits a "theological contemplation," wherein we more directly and intimately contemplate the *Creator*. The acquisition of other virtues helps lead us to this ultimate human operation, giving us a foretaste in this life of the beatific vision of God in the next. In the chapter on Albert's theology, we'll see how he stove for such "cleaving to God."

Chapter 5
Memory Master

> The lector, as well as his assistant, was moreover forbidden to read a written lecture. Everything was committed to memory. Free exposition, such was the rule.
>
> —Fr. Joachim Sighart, Ph.D.[1]

> Whence we say that among all those things which point toward ethical wisdom, the most necessary is trained memory, because from past events we are guided in the present and the future, and not from the converse.
>
> —St. Albert the Great[2]

IN the late 1990s a letter to the editor of the famous high-IQ society's *Mensa Bulletin* asserted that Aristotle had become merely a "historical curiosity." I rejoined in the next issue that if that were true, "then I pray we all become more historically curious!"

There is, you see, an all too common assumption today that the things most worth learning are the things that are hottest off the press. This holds especially true when considering the stuff of science and technology. Every new discovery or invention is lauded, then quickly superseded or outdated as the cutting edge becomes increasingly sharp. But as more and more knowledge from the past comes to be considered passé, we put our own intellects at risk of becoming increasingly blunt.

St. Albert was considered cutting-edge in his time, in many ways ahead of his time, as he helped herald newfound appreciation for scientific investigation. So well-versed was he in the workings of nature and medicine that some believed he was not a scientist but a magician. Yet Albert could not have pushed the envelope of new knowledge if he had not read and meticulously studied what thinkers long before him had already placed within that envelope. Indeed, as we have seen already, Aristotle himself was among those of whom Albert was most "historically curious." Now, Albert lived over 700 years before us, and Aristotle lived over 1,500 years before him, but, as you will see, Albert's historical curiosity led him to cutting-edge knowledge that you and I can put to use today—and yes, I mean *literally today* if you don't set aside the book or fall asleep before this chapter's finished.

Albert spent considerable time and effort focusing his gaze on the pinnacle of God's earthly creation: man himself and in particular his powers of reason and will, those unique faculties that reflect how we alone on Earth are made in the image of God. All of human psychology fell within Albert's purview, including that most practical human power of *memory*.

All too often we shortchange our own capacities for memory. At a very simple level, how many times have you heard someone, or you yourself, say, "I have a terrible memory!" Now, in some ways this could be true. There are actually many different kinds of memory—for things visual or verbal, recent or long past, for material obtained through reading or lecture or that of our own lived experience, to name but a few. Some people are more adept at certain kinds of memory than at others.

Even so, speaking of memory as a whole, to say you have a terrible memory implies that good or poor memory abilities are simply something you *have*, the cards you've been dealt, end of story. But the memory capacities you were born with are in fact only *half* of the story, and now it is time to see how Albert told the whole story—complete with instructions on how to give the story of our own memory capacities a very happy ending.

THE SCIENCE, ART, AND ETHICS OF MEMORY

St. Albert always strove for deeper knowledge both of human nature and of its perfection, of what kind of beings we *are* and of what kind of beings we *could* be, of the powers and capacities within our disposal, and of how best to dispose them. What is memory and how does it work? What is its natural course within the body and soul? How does it work with other mental capacities? These questions are the realm of science. What we *can be*, this is the realm of art, a word that derives from *artifice*—to make. What can we make of our nature? How can we build on it? Can we, for instance, enhance and improve our capacity to remember?

There existed two largely separate veins of ancient golden Greco-Roman wisdom on the science and the "art" of memory, and St. Albert mined them both. Once again we will see that his great contribution was in integration: this time, of Aristotle's theory on the *nature* of human memory with Cicero's writings on memory's *perfection*. But even that was not enough for Albert; he also moved both the science and the art of memory into a whole new sphere of endeavor, transcending both the study of the scientist and lecture hall of the public speaker, and ascending to realm of the daily quest for moral and spiritual perfection within every child of God.

St. Albert wrote *De Bono* (On the Good), his great work in six books on human virtue and morality, during the middle of his mid-career, approximately AD 1240–44.[3] We saw in the last chapter how St. Albert gave vibrant new life to the pursuit of natural virtues within the Christian soul; within its treatment of the parts of the virtue of *prudence*, in the second question of the fourth book, Albert provides his masterful analysis and synthesis of the Aristotelian theory of *what memory is* and the Ciceronian tradition of *how we can improve it*.

As we saw in the quote that began this chapter, St. Albert believed that in exercising prudence, that practical wisdom that guides us toward the means to ethical actions in the present to obtain good results in the future, we must be informed and guided by the previously acquired knowledge and wisdom we hold within our memories. Thus, it's nothing less than a moral duty *to train our memories to become as powerful as they can be.*

"So what *is* memory," you say. "How do we improve it, and how do we use it to serve God and neighbor?" (I thought you'd never ask.)

Regarding the theory of the nature of human memory, in *De Bono* St. Albert addresses Aristotle's model in an article called "What *Memoria* Might Be." There he answers five "objections" to the idea that memory could be part of the virtue of prudence, objections based partly on the idea that prudence is a virtue of the (uniquely human) *rational* or *intellectual soul*, whereas the raw capacity to remember is a power of the *sensitive soul* that we share with lower animals. How could memory, a basic capacity derived from the senses and shared with the beasts, be the most important part of prudence, the natural moral virtue most closely tied to the uniquely human intellectual soul?

Albert replied by noting that although both humans and animals possess the capacity to retain images and impressions of past sense experience, only humans have the additional capacity of *reminiscence*—the ability to use our logical reasoning abilities to search our memories and recall what we seek to recall on purpose. For a simple common example, what do you do when you've lost your keys? Perhaps you try to recall your actions backward in time, seek to remember the pants or the jacket you were wearing when you last had them, or maybe even retrace your actual steps (and if possible, solicit your spouse and kids to help join the search). Furthermore, through our uniquely human capacity to reason, we also possess *the capacity to train our memory* to make easier our future efforts at reminiscence. This is *in habitu cognitivo* (part of cognitive or intellectual training) if our goal is simply to recall theoretical information, but it is *in habitu morali* (part of moral or ethical training) if the goal is to recall practical information of use in guiding our moral actions—and that is the stuff of the virtue of prudence!

In a second article on the question of memory as a part of prudence in *De Bono*, titled "Concerning the Art of Memory," St. Albert really goes to town (that town being Rome), carefully dissecting and reconstructing 21 separate arguments against the very idea that there is such a thing as an "art of memory" (or if there is, whether the one attributed to Cicero is any good).

There was, you see, an ancient system of "artificial" memory that dated back at least to the Greek poet Simonides (ca. 556–468 BC). The ancient Greek manuals on this "art of memory" are lost, though Aristotle makes brief mention of its existence and uses it as an example in several of his books. The oldest memory texts available to Albert (and still to us, for that matter) were two books on rhetoric then attributed to Cicero, *De Inventione* (On Invention) and the *Rhetorica Ad Herennium* (Rhetoric for Herennius). We're not sure to this day just who Herennius was, and although Cicero is still usually listed as the author, we're pretty sure he wasn't. Still, there is nothing in it that runs contrary to the remarks on the art of memory found in his *De Inventione*.

Now, the *Ad Herennium* is a remarkable little book. In my Loeb Classical Library edition,[4] the section addressing memory covers only 25 pages, half with the original Latin and half with the English translation. St. Albert went over this little treatise with a fine-tooth comb and shaped it up so nicely that it served to inspire St. Thomas's brief but monumental analysis of memory as a part of prudence in his *Summa Theologica*.[5]

St. Albert opined that Cicero's (Albert affectionately calls him "Tully") artificial memory method was, simply put, the "best." Along with St. Thomas, he helped perfect and pass down that method to us. But instead of just telling you about it, allow me to demonstrate it for you (and then you can tell me if it's any good or not), complete with adaptations aiding in the perfection of moral prudence. Please set your powers of concentration and imagination on high, then, as we're about to embark on an unusual, though I hope a *memorable*, little trip.

Albert's Art of Memory in *Your* Memory Today

Imagine, if you will, that at some time in the future, up in Heaven (the good Lord willing), you've asked St. Albert the Great himself if he'd mind guiding you through his favorite Gothic cathedral, fresh in all its newly built glory. The kindly learned man, vibrant like never before in his glorified body and pristine white habit, guides you to a massive *front door* of solid gold, and engraved upon it there you see, not a crucifix or a scene from the Bible or from the lives of the saints, but a massive *Webster's Dictionary*. (Don't worry, I'll tell you why a little later.)

Moving along inside into the narthex (*entranceway* or foyer), St. Albert gently grasps your elbow, guiding you around a *giant flask* sitting on the floor, full to the brim with the most delicious looking deep *red wine* that you have ever seen. Passing through an inner door, you turn to your left to dip your hand in the *holy water basin*, only to find, to your surprise, that someone is bathing *a baby* in there! Moving right along, you sit down in the *left rear pew*, moving past a *woman in unfamiliar exotic clothing*, and you note with a start a deep hole right next to you on the other side. Surrounded by stone with a bucket on its edge, you surmise that it is an ancient *water well*.

Next, looking up toward the front of the church at the *lectern* on the left, you see that it is covered, like a *porch*, and stands completely surrounded by a shallow *pool* of water. Glancing up toward the *tabernacle*, you see St. Albert himself open it up, revealing not hosts but *bread* and *fish* (five loaves and two fish to be exact). And there in all His splendor, standing behind the altar, is *Jesus Himself*, teaching the congregation. You also spy, sitting on the altar, an amazing *model replica of the Jewish Temple* of Jerusalem.

Turning next to the wall on the right, you see a *woman* fleeing into the safety of a *confessional booth* as *flying stones* smash against the door. As disturbing as that scene was, you are comforted next as you turn your attention to a magnificent *stained glass window* on the right wall of the cathedral. It depicts a *blind man seeing*, and you can see the sun's rays beaming through his eyes. Last, but not least, your attention is drawn to the back right corner of the cathedral by the braying of sheep! And there you see a kindly *shepherd*, leaning on his staff, as his *sheep* quench their thirst in the *baptismal font*.

Do you have all that? (If not, please read it through one more time.) OK, let's take a little breather. Now, I'm going to set up this next section in the famous question and answer format of the great scholastic treatises, like St. Thomas Aquinas's *Summa Theologica* and St. Albert's own *De Bono*. Here we go:

Question: Whether the preceding exercise had anything to do with the art of memory as a part of prudence.

Objection 1: It would seem that the preceding exercise had nothing to do with the art of memory because it is not clear that we have memorized anything.

Objection 2: It would appear that even if this material were memorized, being of such an odd and nonsensical assortment of images, it would have nothing to do with that virtue of practical wisdom called prudence.

On the contrary, St. Albert himself has written, "that art of memory is best which Tully teaches," that "some will place a church," and further, that "among all those things which point toward ethical wisdom, the most necessary is trained memory."

I answer that because Tully's art of memory has proven successful in practice for over 2,000 years and because Christians who are aware of how Sts. Albert and Thomas Aquinas adapted it to the purposes of the moral life have profited thereby for over 700 years, you, the reader, will soon find that you have memorized ten facts through Tully's art of memory—facts quite relevant to the prudent practice of practical wisdom!

Reply to objection 1: You will see that you have indeed memorized the material within the exercise if you examine the locations and images within the chart below. If necessary, repeat the list a few times, first while looking at the chart and then with your eyes closed. And as you do, create vivid mental pictures within your "mind's eye." To double check on your mastery, I recommend that you also go through the list backward—from ten to one, I mean!

LOCATION	IMAGE
1. Front door	*Dictionary*
2. Entranceway	*Wine flask*
3. Holy water basin	*Baby*
4. Left back pew	*Well*
5. Lectern	*Covered porch and pool*
6. Tabernacle	*Bread and fish*
7. Altar	*Jesus Himself and Temple model*
8. Confessional booth	*Woman fleeing stones*
9. Stained glass window	*Blind man seeing*
10. Baptismal font	*Shepherd watering sheep*

Reply to objection 2: You will see that the material within this exercise is relevant to the practice of the ethical wisdom of the virtue of prudence if you agree that knowledge of the deeds and words of Jesus Christ are worthy to serve as guides to our own behavior in our daily lives. To make this clear, let's take a look at what you've *really* committed to memory.

Do you see now that those odd and quirky images really served the purpose to remind us of things much more profound? The dictionary, a book full of words, should remind us of "the Word made flesh," Jesus Christ Himself. The wine flask reminds us of Christ's first miracle, turning water to wine at the wedding feast at Cana. The baby reminds us we must be "born anew." The well reminds us how Jesus revealed Himself as Christ to the woman from Samaria, since he came to redeem not only the Jews. The porch and the pool remind us of Jesus's miracle of healing the paralyzed man at the pool with five porticoes (porches). The bread and fish remind us of the miracle of the multiplication of the loaves and fishes. Jesus at the altar with the temple reminds us that Jesus went to the Temple of Jerusalem to preach his message. The woman and the stones reminds us of that

Location (Chapter # from St. John's Gospel)	Image	Gospel Lesson
1. Front door	*Dictionary*	"In the beginning was the Word, and the Word was with God."[6]
2. Entranceway	*Wine flask*	Jesus turns water to wine.
3. Holy water basin	*Baby*	"Unless one is born anew, he cannot see the kingdom of God."[7]
4. Left back pew	*Woman and well*	Jesus meets Samaritan woman at Jacob's well.
5. Lectern	*Covered porch and pool*	Jesus heals the paralyzed man at the pool.
6. Tabernacle	*Bread and fish*	Jesus multiplies the loaves and fishes.
7. Altar	*Jesus Himself and temple model*	Jesus teaches at the Temple.
8. Confessional booth	*Woman fleeing stones*	Jesus forgives the adulteress.
9. Stained glass window	*Blind man seeing*	Jesus gives the blind man sight.
10. Baptismal font	*Shepherd watering sheep*	"I am the good shepherd. The good shepherd lays down his life for his sheep."[8]

dramatic event where Jesus refused to condemn the adulteress yet commanded her to sin no more. The stained glass window depicts another glorious miracle in which Jesus gave the blind man sight. This is also a reminder of the Sacraments, since Jesus used material things (spittle and clay in this case) to work the healing. Finally, the good shepherd reminds us of Jesus Himself and how he gave his life for His sheep—those sheep including you and me.

Note also the role of the *numbers* of the locations. In this particular demonstration, they represent the chapter numbers within the Gospel of St. John in which these events are found. This means that *you* now know one major event or lesson within the first ten chapters of St. John's Gospel—in order!

So do you see now what St. Albert meant by "placing a church?" Building a series of locations enhances our power to remember things well and in precise order. And indeed, once a series of locations is well learned, they can be used again and again for brand new sets of material. In that way, you can build up all kinds of cathedrals in your mind to house all kinds of information relevant to the Faith, which can guide your prudent, moral daily living.

This is the 2,000-year-old memory technique called the "method of *loci*" (locations) that Albert painstakingly gleaned from the imperfect, partially corrupted editions of the *Ad Herennium* available to him.[9]

By adding additional places, you can easily store even more information. With 21 locations, for example, you could store a key event from every chapter in St. John's Gospel and then go back and add more of the key events and lessons in each chapter, "writing them on the tablet of your heart."[10] In *Memorize the Faith!* I used 60 different locations to house hundreds of facts and precepts of the Faith, such as the Ten Commandments, virtues, vices, beatitudes, rosary mysteries, Stations of the Cross, books of the Bible, and on and on. The possibilities for expansion are limitless! By the way, I chose the Gospel of St. John as my example because St. Albert once lectured on this gospel, at the pope's invitation, at the papal court in Rome. We'll come across that story again later, in the context of yet another

Albertine legend, in chapters on Albert as a provincial of his order and as a "charging champion" of the Faith.

We'll also see more of Albert's own prodigious powers of memory in action elsewhere in this book. Let us conclude here by giving him due credit as a "medieval memory master," advancing Christian civilization's understanding of the power of memory and building us a bridge to ancient practical wisdom on increasing and refining that power. It is fair to say that he and St. Thomas rewrote the book on memory. In fact, they rewrote it so well, they no longer needed books to remember it!

GREAT IDEA #5: THE VIRTUE OF MEMORY

St. Albert advanced the art of memory from the realm of cognition to the realm of moral behavior, from the orator's podium to the preacher's lectern, from a method for improving the mind to a method for perfecting the soul. Albert's art of memory still retained all of its prior powers as an aid to thinking, academic achievement, and public speaking. But just as *artificial memory* builds upon *natural memory*, Albert's approach built upon *both* what we might well call *supernatural memory*, since he saw memory as a part of prudence, that is, finding the right means to right ends. For St. Albert, those ends or goals must of course accord with God's truths as represented in the theology and morals of the Catholic Church.

For Albert, then, memory has literally become a virtue. *The Catechism of the Catholic Church* tells us "a virtue is a habitual and firm disposition to do the good." Further, "the virtuous person tends toward the good *with all his sensory and spiritual powers* . . . The goal of a virtuous life is to become like God."[11] Training our memories then, utilizes our sensory and intellectual powers in order to make us more like God—the ultimate embodiment of truth and goodness.

St. Albert knew well that virtuous dispositions are strengthened through the *practice* of virtuous acts. So here is one simple practical suggestion to enhance your own virtue of memory. Read the five brief chapters of the epistle of St. James, a letter rich in practical advice on bringing faith alive through the good works of charity. Place two or three images representing the key ideas of each chapter in the first five locations of our imaginary church. Then, during morning prayer time each day for the next week, recall those key ideas and find some way to put at least one into practice that day.

PART II

DOER

Chapter 6

Docile Dominican

As long as the Dominican Order can nurture at its bosom
scholars in any field of knowledge—for all knowledge
can lead to God—as long as it can generate a race of
preachers who, by solid dispensation of the Word, can
fortify men for the road that leads to God, it will not
hesitate or apologize for the frankly intellectual bias
given it by given it by Albert and his four associates on
the Commission of Valenciennes.

—Thomas Schwertner, O.P.[1]

The Dominican path—the Dominican way—is only one
path among many. But it is a path which is truly "broad
and joyous."

—Paul Murray, O.P.[2]

W E find ourselves now embarking on the second part of our
examination of the life and lessons of our great-souled man.
Our emphasis shifts from St. Albert the *thinker* to St. Albert the *doer*,
from *he who contemplates* to *he who produces fruits*. As we shall
see, however, this is not a complete change of direction but merely a
shift of emphasis—since thinking and doing often go hand in hand.
Indeed, Albert believed that we are best able to *do* the good only
when we come to *know* with certainty what is good. In this section,
then, we will focus on the fruits that sprang from Albert's passionate
love for truth, wherever he found it.

I'll let you know right from the get-go that there's no way I can write this chapter from an objective and unbiased standpoint. You see, I was educated by (it pains me a little to say it) "penguins"— the term my childhood buddies and I used in the 1960s and '70s to refer to those devout, dedicated, and disciplined Dominican Sisters of Springfield, Illinois, beclad in their immaculate black-and-white habits. For nine years of my childhood and adolescence I was guided along by many good sisters who tread the path of St. Dominic. It would take me several decades, however, to begin to grasp just how "broad and joyous" is the path they follow!

Just last summer, 34 years since I was last in their charge, my family and I had the great joy to share Mass and brunch with a group of those sisters. (With some trepidation I presented copies of my books to my eighth-grade English teacher, fearful she would detect grammatical infelicities that had slipped past the watchful eyes of my editor.) In their chapel, among the beautiful artistic renderings of saints that adorn its back wall, is one of St. Albert the Great. So indulge me a little, as we look at the works of St. Albert the doer, if I draw here and there from the lessons I learned from some of his very special spiritual descendants.

IMBIBING THE DOMINICAN SPIRIT

In this section we'll examine how and why St. Albert came to be a Dominican priest, and we'll witness some of the greatest deeds he performed for that order. In the next chapter, for instance, we'll focus on the foundational task and goal of the Order of Preachers—that of preaching to draw souls to Christ. For now, though, I'd like to provide just a taste of the Dominican spiritual charism that so attracted St. Albert and so guided his thoughts and works. Here I stand in great debt to the insights provided in Father Paul Murray's book: *The New Wine of Dominican Spirituality: A Drink Called Happiness*.

I almost labeled this section "Eat, Drink, and be Hilarious (Again)" because it touches on a theme from my book *Unearthing Your Ten*

Talents, which mentions St. Thomas Aquinas's recommendation to drink alcohol in moderation "to the point of hilarity." Among his many inspiring insights on Dominican spirituality, drawn from the writings of great Dominican saints and theologians, Father Murray compares the Dominicans' joy in God to joyous inebriation from fine wine. This is a common scriptural metaphor—see, for example, Jeremiah 23:9—and many Dominican writings magnify the joy of wine and its connection to the love of God:[3]

- "They all drank as much as they wanted, encouraged by St. Dominic, who kept on saying, 'Drink up, my daughters!' At that time there were 104 sisters there and they all drank as much as they wanted" (Blessed Cecelia).
- "The strength of wine . . . gives a person a lift . . . brings delight and puts a man at ease" (Blessed Jordan of Saxony).
- "The one who makes his hearers drunk with the word of God will himself be made drunk with a draft of manifold blessing" (Humbert of Romans).
- "Do not neglect prayer . . . and remain often in your cell if you would be admitted to the wine-cellar" (St. Thomas Aquinas).
- "Let us behave like the drunkard who doesn't think of himself, but only of the wine that has been drunk and of the wine that remains to be drunk" (St. Catherine of Siena).

A nature-lover like Albert would be right at home in company of the wine-loving Dominicans! They knew as he did that God's creation is good and that he intends for us to be happy in enjoying (within reasonable limits) its bounty. Indeed, one of their early tasks was to combat the Albigensian heresy, which proclaimed that the material world of creation was evil (and that Jesus, therefore, could not have been incarnated in real human flesh). Drinking wine also expresses the expansiveness and joy of the Dominican soul. Their job was to preach the good news to man. So who is likely to believe the news is good if its bearer is rigid, and narrow, and joyless?

At a much deeper level, of course, "wine" and "intoxication" refer in a mystical sense to the "new wine" of the Spirit. When the Blessed Mother remarks, in John 2:3, "They have no wine," she is referring not only to a wedding party that had run dry but to a human race bereft of the interior joy and life that only God could give them.

The religious order that spoke to Albert's heart (at the prompting of Mother Mary herself, in some recountings) was full of men and women so grateful for the beneficence of God's creation that they could see it as good, seek to study it to the core, and become intoxicated by its beauty and goodness yet never forget the deeper levels of meaning and mystery that always lead us away from created things and back to the Creator.

BLESSED JORDAN ANOINTS EUROPE WITH THE FINEST OF COLOGNE

And now for the story of how Albert became a Dominican. Blessed Jordan of Saxony (1190–1237), the Dominican patron of vocations, succeeded St. Dominic himself as the Master General of the Order of Preachers in 1222. Because of the power of his preaching, the magnetism of his charity, and the humor in his heart,[4] he was able to rake them in to the religious life like few before him or since. Some say he drew in more than a thousand vocations to the order during his 15 years as general. Among those enticed by this "wonderful charmer of souls"[5] were Hugh of St. Cher, later a cardinal and producer of the world's first biblical concordance, and Humbert of Romans, himself later general of the order and collaborator on its distinctive liturgy. But the biggest catch for this fisher of men was the future Albert the Great.

Soon after a visit to Padua in 1223, Blessed Jordan wrote to Blessed Diana d'Andalo about his latest recruits, specifically mentioning "two sons of German noblemen; the one a high official; the second truly noble in mind and body, enjoying great revenues. We hope that many similarly endowed will follow their examples."[6] One of these noble young men was likely our Albert. His choice was not an easy one: his uncle, dreaming of worldly success for his young charge, was strongly opposed to Albert's interactions with the new mendicant order and made him wait before making his decision. Albert too had reason to hesitate. Though he cared nothing for following his ancestors' footsteps in service to the emperor, he was aware of his own passion for knowledge and experience of things of the world, for animals and architecture, for medicine and science, for the philosophy of the Greeks, and he feared, like many others, that this thirst for the knowledge of the things of this world might draw him away from devotion to Christ.

And here enters another Albertine legend! Albert had a dream that he had entered the order but left it soon after. Upon awakening he rejoiced that his dream had foretold for him that which he had been fearing. But later that same day he attended a sermon in which Master Jordan declared that the devil sometimes subtly deceives men by telling them in their dreams that they will enter the order but not persevere! Albert approached the master and asked how he had read his heart. Jordan comforted him; Albert cast aside his fears and soon after became a Dominican for life.

Once in the order, Albert kept far too busy to even have a moment to consider leaving his priestly office (though, as we shall see, at the pope's request he did for a time leave the convent for episcopal office). Let's consider further exactly why the Dominican order provided such perfect soil for growing greatness of soul.

ACTS OF THE MEDIEVAL APOSTLES

Albert could have become a secular priest and indeed later was made a bishop for a time, though not on his own initiative. He could have sought out a comfortable and well-established monastic order or could even have joined the devout and merry band of "fools for Christ" in the new order of St. Francis. As providence would have it, though, young Albert would choose an order whose primary mission was, and remains, "preaching, and the salvation of souls,"[7] to be achieved by means of the vows of obedience, chastity, and poverty;

by communal life with monastic observances; by the recitation of the Divine Office; and by the study of sacred truth.

The religious vows of obedience, chastity, and poverty freed the friars to follow Christ with all their heart, mind, strength, and soul. Sts. Albert and Thomas would write of obedience as a component of "observance," a virtue related to justice, whereby we give to each his rightful due; in this case, by paying honor and respect to those who excel us in some way. Albert, like all Dominicans, paid such due by vowing obedience to his prior at the local level, to his provincial at the regional level, and to the master general of the entire order. This vow fostered a spirit of selflessness and made available all of one's talents for the good of the order, which is to say, for the good of the Good News.

Chastity relates to the virtue of temperance that reins in our desires for earthly goods. In taking a vow of chastity, Albert embraced celibacy and rejected married family life in order to give himself fully to his order, thereby freeing himself from worldly cares and allowing him to share the fruits of his contemplation with full and undivided attention. Indeed, the leader of the first apostles told them that purity of heart would enable them to see God.[8] How much greater the preaching of preachers with eyes only for God and how much greater trust from those who saw and heard them preach?

Poverty, too, replaces desires for the earthly with desires for the heavenly. In vowing to forsake ownership of worldly goods, Albert, though born to earthly wealth and nobility, would attain the riches of a far greater kingdom.[9]

Albert chose to live in a community that embraced many monastic observances that St. Dominic acquired from the traditional practices of the Benedictines, from simple religious habits and communal life to practices like periods of fasting, silence, penance, night vigils, and more. These would serve to honor God and to focus St. Albert in all his being on doing God's work, and later, in training others to do the same. This communal life also trained Albert to see Christ within his religious brothers.[10]

Recitation of the Divine Office or Liturgy of the Hours was and is another cornerstone of Dominican spirituality. The Dominicans sought to imitate the Apostles in their zeal for prayer as well as preaching. The Twelve had continued ancient Jewish practices of praying at *matins* (midnight); *terce,* or third hour (9 a.m.); *sext,* or sixth hour (noon); and *nones,* or ninth hour (3 p.m.).[11] By Albert's time, this schedule of prayers had become more elaborate, including as well four additional prayer times: *lauds* at dawn, *prime* at 6 a.m., *vespers* in the evening, and *compline* before retiring but still had its basis in the Psalms. These prayers were called the Divine Office from the Latin *officiis* for "duties." These regular prayers, then, were duties owed to God, following St. Paul's exhortation to "pray always." These periods of communal prayer, along with daily Mass, helped Albert to follow in the footsteps of St. Paul himself, as a learned man of many travels and powerful writings and preachings of the gospel of Christ.

Sacred study was the last pillar upon which the spiritual house of the sons of St. Dominic was built. In a time of rampant heresy, of threats from rediscovered pagan philosophies, and of Islam's fierce and fervent expansion, an effective preacher needed great knowledge as well as holiness and courage. In Albert's day the Dominicans played a major role in the development of the European university, with St. Albert himself and his young charge St. Thomas eventually becoming the most universal of all the universities' doctors.[12]

All of these fundamental practices of the Dominican order— their vows of obedience, chastity, and poverty, their communal life, monastic practices, recitation of the Divine Office and participation in daily Eucharist in the holy Mass, and their dedicated study of sacred truth—were means to preach the good news and win souls to God, to share the fruits of their contemplation that would lead their neighbors to eternal salvation. Surely then, when St. Dominic responded to God's call to send forth his friar-preachers among the nations to use their minds to reach men's hearts, he could not have imagined a more perfect Dominican fisher of men than that young broad-shouldered German whom Blessed Jordan had first caught in his net.

GREAT IDEA #6: JOY!

Joy is not a virtue distinct from charity, but an act or effect of charity: for which reason it is number among the Fruits.

—St. Thomas Aquinas[13]

Albert was what we might call today a "nature lover," and the legends of this love go back to his childhood days and his great enthusiasm for falconry. There is also the story, told by some German locals and early biographers, of a certain magnificent and high-spirited "White Horse of Lauingen" that could be tamed by no man but would peacefully follow wherever the boy Albert would lead him.

Now, both Albert and Thomas knew joy, both as a concept and as an actual experience. Joy is an effect or an end-state resulting from love. When we *love* something good we *desire* it until we possess it, and when we possess the object of our love, then we experience *joy*. (And on the contrary, when we *hate* something evil we *fear* it if it has not come upon us, and we feel *sorrow* when it has.) Joy then is a delightful result of love. St. Thomas said that joy is to desire as rest is to movement. Could perhaps that legendary white horse of Lauingen have sensed the calm and restful state of joy in the presence of young Albert?

God made us for joy. St. Paul tells us that "the kingdom of God does not mean food and drink but righteousness and peace and joy in the Holy Spirit."[14] The highest joy, of course, is the result of the highest love, the love of God in charity, and through this love, we can be certain that St. Albert's joy was indeed very great.

Chapter 7

Prudent Preacher

He is truly zealous for souls who by holy contemplation and fervent desire, by tears and prayers, by night-
watchings and fasts, by preaching and hearing of
confessions, by wise counsel, salutary correction, and
other good works labors for the salvation of souls.

—St. Albert the Great[1]

Saint Albert's great purpose in life, as we have seen, was
to lead men to God.

—Maurus M. Niehus, O.P., S.T.L[2]

IN the days of Albert's youth at the dawn of the 13th century, the
quality of preaching was at a low ebb throughout Christendom.
The Church was closely intertwined with the feudal system and many
of the higher clergy were feudal lords, immersed in managing their
worldly affairs, and often of less than impeccable moral integrity.
The lower ranking clergy were too often just ignorant. Parish priests
were supposed to comment on the Our Father and the Creed each
Sunday but preaching would not become a regular and obligatory
part of Mass for another three centuries. Preaching was the official
province of the bishops, but many of them, so wrapped up in the
world, declined to exercise that duty and privilege.

When the Saints Went Marching Out

Enter not one but *two* saintly men of God. In 1209, a humble former soldier heard a sermon on Matthew 10:9, in which Christ enjoins his 12 disciples to go forth into the world and preach the news of his salvation, taking "no gold, nor silver, nor copper in your belts." This man became what some would call "a second Christ," as he assembled his own band of followers embracing poverty and a life of itinerant evangelization. Shortly thereafter, with the blessing of Pope Innocent III, St. Francis of Assisi's *Ordo Fratrum Minorum*, the Order of Friars Minor, the Franciscans, had been formed.

It is considered likely that St. Francis himself met another young man on fire for Christ when in 1215 he attended the Fourth Lateran Council in Rome. One of the themes of that council was the need for good preaching, and that young man, Dominic de Guzman, would go on to found a great order of preachers, as known for their learning as were the Franciscans for their poverty. He sought to imitate Christ in his wisdom[3] and in his zeal to spread the gospel throughout the world.

It was said that young Dominic was never seen without a book, often the Bible (though later he would sell all his books for the poor), and he knew that the Church was under attack intellectually from various heresies (like the aforementioned Albigensians) as well as by misinterpretations of rediscovered Greek philosophy. He knew that to win men's hearts to God he had to equip not only his heart with love but his mind with knowledge. He would build on the intellectual treasures amassed by the Benedictine monks in their monasteries and take to the streets, where too often the people lived in sad ignorance of the message of their Saviour.

In 1216, one year after that Fourth Lateran Council in Rome, Pope Honorius III would approve the *Ordo Praedicatorum*, the Order of Preachers, the Dominicans. As we saw in the last chapter, this was the new order that God led young Albert to join. What better possible match for this young man's burgeoning powers?

ALBERT THE GREAT AND THE DOGS OF GOD

The Dominicans, as we have seen, had two special missions from the start: they were devoted to contemplation and to sharing its fruits with others. A novel characteristic of both new orders (called *mendicant* orders, since they lived in poverty and begged for their livings) was that they were not bound to one location or one bishop; instead they traveled freely as dictated by need.

There were critics. Some considered scientific and philosophical learning a threat to faith. Others argued against the freedom to travel outside of a parish or cloister, feeling this would allow the devil to snare young religious with worldly temptations. Albert was no doubt aware of the criticisms, just as he was conscious of the potential for secular learning to crowd out the spiritual life. But he was not dissuaded, even when—as one legend tells—a holy monk visited him to try to talk him out of the Dominicans and into cloistered life instead. That "monk," it turned out, was the devil in disguise.

But what of Albert at the pulpit? What on earth could the most brilliant scientific mind of his age, a man who deduced the spherical shape of the earth by mathematical calculation, a man who corrected *Aristotle's* errors, have to say to the common man and woman of the Middle Ages?

Albert's masterwork as a teacher, St. Thomas Aquinas himself, noted that "a characteristic of one possessing science is his ability to teach."[4] Albert possessed science to an unequalled degree, and with it the matching ability to preach not just on theology but in areas of morality and virtue. Thus we can be sure he had great interest in, and many wise prescriptions for, ordinary people and the practical problems of their daily lives.

Let's look at a few examples that show Albert's care and concern for his common neighbors (and his homespun wit as well).

In a famous sermon on the gospel story of Lazarus and Dives, the rich man, St. Albert focuses in on Luke 16:19, where dogs come to lick Lazarus's sores. It seems that at the time the Dominicans were sometimes popularly referred to as "watchdogs of the Lord" or "hounds of God"—a play on *Domini* ("of the Lord") and *canes* ("dogs"). In his sermon, Albert joins right in the fun (and wisdom): "The roving dogs are the Order of Preachers who do not wait at their homes for the poor but go out to them and lick the ulcers of their sins having in their mouths the bark of preaching . . . Every good preacher is a living dog because he has the grace of a bark in his preaching, of reproof in his tooth and of healing in the counsel of his tongue."[5] As you can see, despite his brilliance Albert's sermons were very down to earth—though always pointing toward Heaven! Though he was even then being called "great," he gently humiliates himself in order to make his message relevant to his listeners. Though a master of the ancient arts of rhetoric, in his sermons he characteristically eschews flashy, ostentatious gimmicks that would draw attention toward himself and away from the gospel.

One favorite predicatory theme of Albert's was that of medicine and the healing of disease. Since medicine was essentially applied biology, Albert the scientist abounded in medical knowledge for a man of his day, and he put the knowledge to work for spiritual ends as well. He may have also taken inspiration from the Stoic philosophers he knew and loved, who called their philosophies "medicine for men's minds" and called themselves "healers of souls." Incarnationally minded in everything he did, Albert's preaching was, as Father Schwertner put it, "a practical attempt to get at men's souls through their bodies."[6]

ALBERT'S ART OF PRUDENT PREACHING

Though, as we soon will see, Albert's duties would sometimes draw him away from his teaching, all his life he never ceased preaching. This was why Albert burned with such passion for knowledge of things earthly and divine: so that he might save souls and lead them to Heaven. It is reported that Albert actually prepared a manual on the *Art of Preaching*, though tragically it has not reached us through the centuries. We do have many of his sermons, though (unfortunately not in readily available English translations), including a series of 32 sermons on the Eucharist that were thought for a time to have been penned by St. Thomas Aquinas.

As for Albert's preaching style, Fr. Schumpp tells us that he wasn't "so powerful and eloquent a speaker as Bertold of Ratisbon, his contemporary; nor was his pulpit like that of the latter surrounded by thousands, so that churches could not contain his audiences; his words were simpler, plainer, calmer as is proper for a man of learning."[7] In contrast to his university teaching, where Albert packed in learned men from all over Europe, in his preaching to locals of diverse intellectual capacities and backgrounds Albert tailored his messages to suit. Albert's simple style was deliberate, his humility outshining his intellectual brilliance when it came to preaching the good news to the masses.

Hear Albert himself in words as homely as they are profound: "The Blessed Virgin Mary wrapped the Word of the Father in humble bands to teach us that the divine Word should be clothed by preachers in simple language rather than in rhetorical."[8] Indeed, to see that the master's greatest pupil had absorbed a similar lesson, I suggest that you compare St. Thomas's awesome and scholarly *Summa Theologica* to his delightfully clear and simple sermons.[9]

When Albert preached, it was never all about self-aggrandizement—it was about humbly and faithfully communicating the gospel. Nonetheless, his preaching exploits were not without their own legends. One tale was told by the citizens of Ratisbon, centuries after Albert's time, that when a heretical preacher attempted to deliver a sermon from a pulpit he had once occupied, he was instantly struck dumb and did not regain his voice until he had moved to another pulpit.

Such was Albert's reputation for spiritual wisdom that one time even Brother Bertold went to him for spiritual advice, asking, "What Christian work is most pleasing to God?" Whereupon Albert replied, "If one sees his fellow-man in great labor and distress and consoles him by word and work and assists him as much as possible, that before

God, is the most pleasing work a man can perform."[10] This calls to my mind the parable of the Good Samaritan. He who would inherit eternal life must love the Lord with all his heart, soul, strength, and mind, and his neighbor as himself. This love of the neighbor is shown not only by good wishes but also by good deeds, or as St. John had put it, "Let us not love in word or speech but in deed and truth."[11]

Albert's sermons were abundant in references to scripture, assuming a familiarity with the Bible in his educated lay listeners—centuries before the invention of the printing press—that might give us a start today. In remarking on a collection of his sermons intended as examples, Albert described them as "ordered and based on Holy Scriptures, a whole harvest of sermons could be produced, God willing. There could be found now in one place, now in another, material for strengthening faith, directing souls in the Christian life, and nourishing their devotions."[12]

Albert's sermons on the gospels, on the saints, and on other topics were elegant, simple, direct, and informative; they enlightened the mind and inspired the flesh to action. They typically consisted of three parts:

1. A short and straightforward *literal explanation* of a scriptural passage (usually from the New Testament).

2. An *allegorical and mystical interpretation* of the passage—see for example our previous example of the parable of Lazarus and Dives, on which Albert explores the contrast between Lazarus's eventual generous and eternal reward in Heaven for his painful and hard-won virtue here on Earth and Dives's eventual just and everlasting punishment for the soft and easy pleasures, luxuries, and vices he cultivated while in this world.

3. A *summary* of his message in simple, bold, and straightforward language. If such was the fate of the soft and gluttonous Dives, what then might be the eternal destiny set aside for those among us who sin against God's commandments with acts of adultery, murder, blasphemy, thievery,

and more? Taking a cue from the great Eastern church father, St. John Chrysostom (the "Golden-Mouthed"), this take-home message was often then cast in the form of a simple, manly, and memorable *prayer* that God would grant unto us the spiritual fruits that should accrue from pondering and applying his sacred lessons.

We can clearly see, then, that the Albertine homily was neither an academic discourse nor a shallow excursion but a swift and direct course to knowledge and illumination, along with means for remembering its message and putting it into action. In Albert's own words, "The preacher must take what matter suits him [on each subject.] He should limit himself to developing one or two points and leave the rest to another time."[13]

ALBERT'S LESSON FOR TODAY'S HOMILIST

St. Albert would surely have much to teach those who preach in our modern-day parishes. As a visitor to many lands and a preacher to persons from all walks of life, he'd have much to say about the necessity of tailoring sermons to suit the needs and abilities of the audience. As a memory master he could certainly share tips and tricks for helping listeners to absorb what they're hearing and recall it later. But perhaps above all, Albert could teach modern priests and deacons how to communicate the glory and grandeur of the Faith, how never to downplay or be ashamed of the truths of the Church. Albert knew how to reach people "where they were," but he also knew he had to inspire them to become *more* than they were, to challenge them with the gospel to grow wiser and holier. He knew that to be a preacher is to be God's instrument—a high and humbling calling.

GREAT IDEA #7: EVANGELIZATION

The four evangelists tell us that after Christ's death and Resurrection, and before his Ascension into Heaven, he issued a great call to Peter and the disciples to feed his sheep, to make new disciples, and to spread the good news of his life and his works for our salvation unto all the nations, indeed unto all of creation.

There is a sense in which all of Christ's disciples are called to be evangelists, to spread the good news of Christ through our words and our actions. Still, we are blessed to have "specialists" in this field. We've seen, for example, how the medieval Franciscans and Dominicans took to heart this call to preach and spread the gospel. In modern times, we have coined the phrase "televangelists" for preachers who spread the news far and wide through the means of television. The word television itself is one of those odd Greek-Latin combinations—from the Greek *tele,* meaning "at a distance," and the Latin *videre,* meaning "to see."

Speaking of televangelists, it occurs to me that there are great similarities between St. Albert and a modern evangelist who is currently on the road to sainthood. This man was also a learned professor—in fact his knowledge of the great scholastics and their perennial philosophy and wisdom about the nature of mankind enabled him to point out to the modern masses the pitfalls of godless systems of psychology and politics like Freudian psychiatry and Marxist Communism. This wonderful preacher also had a special devotion to Mary, and he too was a bishop. He influenced me in my youth and many others to this day. I'm talking of course about the perhaps future *Saint* Archbishop Fulton J. Sheen.

Chapter 8

Providential Provincial

Albert was another Dominic, a second founder of the
Order of the German Empire. He is the first who appears
to us here as having received from God not only the gift
of knowledge and wisdom, but even the rare talent of
administration (*chrisma gubernationis*).

—Joachim de Sighart[1]

Brother Albert, Provincial, and the servant of all, to all
our beloved Brethren, the Priors and Convents of the
German Province: health and brotherly charity in Christ.

—St. Albert the Great[2]

THERE is an old saying of dubious veracity that "those who can,
do, and those who can't, *teach!*" The college courses I used to
teach on developmental psychology were also part of the curricu-
lum for secondary education students, so I become familiar with (and
amused by) a further refinement of the adage, namely, "those who
can neither do nor teach—*teach teachers!*"

Well, if there was ever an exception to prove these rules, his great
name was Albert.

We have seen clearly enough that Albert could teach and Albert
could preach and Albert could write, and later we'll even see that
Albert could fight, though he always preferred to settle things peacefully. What we'll see in this chapter is that this great thinker was
also quite the doer—particularly in his role as Dominican provincial,

charged with instilling in over a thousand good men and women life, discipline, growth, and fire for Christ.

CRUSHING THE HEAD OF THE SERPENT

In the year 1254, a Bavarian member of a regular religious order received a vision while praying at St. Peter's in Rome. A monstrous serpent had writhed into the basilica, with horrible hissing that filled not only the church but all of Rome. Just then arrived a man, clothed in the habit of the Order of Preachers, whose name was revealed to him as Albert. The serpent attacked Albert, encircling him head to toe in its muscular, slithering coils. The friar burst free, though, and made his way to the pulpit, whereupon he read from the Gospel of St. John up to the words *"Verbum caro factum est et habitavit in nobis"* ("And the Word became flesh and dwelled among us," 1:14). At these words the serpent fled and ceased its hissing. When our great Dominican arrived in Rome that same year, the man told Albert of his vision, but Albert could not discern its meaning.

HIS FLESH IS CLOTHED OF WORMS

In that same year of 1254, according to the records of the Dominican provincial chapter of the ancient city of Worms,[3] Germany, "Master Albert, a highly esteemed instructor,"[4] was elected provincial in charge of the massive and burgeoning province of Germany, extending at that time as far north as the English Sea, as far east as Poland, and as far south as the whole of Austria and Switzerland; it included regions such as Swabia, Serbia, Bavaria and the Rhineland, Alsace, Holland, Brabant, Silesia, Flanders, Frisia, Westphalia, Hesse, Saxony, and other contiguous lands and cities. Albert's authority for the next 3 years would extend to over 40 convents and smaller establishments.

The sheer vastness of this territory is what gave rise to Sighart's description of Albert as a second Dominic, founding a "German

empire" of preaching friars. It also gave rise to many Albertine letters. It required Herculean labors for a man of 50-plus years to travel
in person to all of those locales and to clean out their stables so to
speak, and writing letters helped him multiply those labors. Still,
our great saint was always on the go, walking in rough wooden
shoes throughout his vast territory. (We take note that he was unsur-
prisingly fit, "of noble stature, and endowed with great physical
strength. His body was well-proportioned, and perfectly fitted for
all the fatigues of God's service."[5]) Often in the company of his
young friend and disciple, the budding theologian Ulric of Strasbourg, Albert traversed the rough terrain of what perhaps we might
call his "Holy Germanic Empire."

A Firm yet Loving Leadership

Albert took very seriously the vows that he and his religious brothers made before God—including poverty and obedience. We retain
the letters in which he enforced the Dominican rule that the religious
would travel by foot, never by horse, mule, or carriage, except under
certain specified conditions—such as a medical emergency or an
assignment of special urgency requiring haste. Indeed, he imposed
a penance upon the Prior of Worms, including seven days on bread
and water along with prescribed Psalters and disciplines, for using
a carriage, and one on the Prior of Minden, including five days on
bread and water, along with Psalters and disciplines, for arriving at a
chapter conference on horseback!

And again on behalf of Lady Poverty, Albert forbade the Dominicans in his province to carry or hoard money. In a punishment that
must sound harsh to the soft and fleshy modern ear, when he learned
that undisclosed money and clothing had been found among the
effects of a deceased lay brother at Pettau, in the diocese of Salzburg,
Albert had his body exhumed and buried in unconsecrated ground.[6]
Note, though, that in this and all matters Albert exacted no discipline from his brothers that he did not also lay upon himself. (He

had renounced a noble patrimony to join the order, after all.) As we shall soon see, even as bishop, Albert voluntarily retained many of the Dominican disciplines. Albert would never forget to live that sermon of rich Dives and poor Lazarus that he had preached so well. It should be mentioned also that the Dominican rule, patterned after that of St. Augustine, was not as rigid as some. Also, Albert sought to add no new restrictions, and though he enforced the existing rule with rigor, he did so also with impartiality and gentleness. His zeal was evidently appreciated and rewarded, as the German province flourished with great numbers of new recruits.

Albert was also concerned for the morals and the souls of his Dominican brothers. Lest the benefits of his reforms die with him, Albert reiterated the admonition of the previous General Chapter requiring Dominicans to confess their sins to their prior once yearly, so that he should know the state of their souls. This paralleled the decree of the Lateran Council of 1215 that all Catholics should confess once a year to their parish priest.[7] A popular confessor himself, Albert was known for his serious but just penances.

In his nearly four years as provincial, Albert would establish three new convents for men—at Straussberg in Thuringen in 1254, at Seehausen in Altmark in 1255, and at Rostock in 1256. He also enlarged others, including those at Cologne and Utrecht. We'll visit the convent for women he established in "Paradise" itself when we arrive at Chapter 13.

Even while assuming the demands of a provincial, Albert was ever the saint and the scientist. His first stop at every priory was the chapel for prayer. Later in the evening, when official duties were done for the day, Albert would be found in the library, diligently reading and writing. Indeed, he cites in his own books many medieval literary treasures of those priories that have been lost to us and have not been cited since. Always striving to serve, he left many of his own writings behind him as well. Much like St. Paul in his travels had left behind a trail of tents, St. Albert left behind a trail of texts. Such intellectual and spiritual endeavors were surely this great saint's greatest calling.

Eventually the sons of St. Dominic decided to free this great mind for his scientific, theological, and academic pursuits. It is reported that "on account of his matchless knowledge he was released from the office of provincial by the General Chapter of 1257."[8] But as we'll see soon, the Bishop of Rome had some plans of his own.

AN ALBERTINE LEGACY OF PERSONAL PIETY AND APOSTOLIC ZEAL

So then, what was left behind when the perhaps reluctant administrator became once again the zealous scientist, theologian, and teacher? Albert had sought to expand the order, and this he achieved. He sought to help perfect the interior life of his brother Dominicans, and this too he did, through the loving enforcement and embodiment the Dominican vows and rule, and through the promotion of the Sacrament of confession within every priory. At the Chapter of Efurt in 1256 he strove to perfect the Dominicans in their primary call to preaching, decreeing that no one could preach outside his convent walls until after he had done so frequently within them. Albert also strove to fire the apostolic zeal of his order, sending Dominican apostles to the farther reaches of Europe still immersed in pagan ways, and in 1256 he urged the priors and friars of the German province to missionary work in foreign lands.

Provincial Albert also stood as a devoted servant of the Holy Pontiff. In 1256, Pope Alexander IV summoned Albert to Anagni, the seat of the papacy at the time. It seems certain secular teachers from the University of Paris had been spreading venomous stories about Dominicans and Franciscans of the university. We'll look at the details of this encounter in Chapter 15, but for now let it suffice to note that St. Albert eventually sent the detractors slithering out of town, and the pope was so impressed with Albert's learning and eloquence that he retained him to preach to the papal court about the Gospel of St. John—"*Verbum caro factum est et habitavit in nobis*" and more!

GREAT IDEA #8: FRIENDSHIP

Friendship was an important subject for classical philosophers such as Aristotle and Cicero, was addressed in the Wisdom literature of the Old Testament, and was portrayed through examples in both testaments, from the powerful enduring friendship of David and Jonathan to that between Jesus Christ and St. John, his beloved disciple. St. Augustine reflected on his friendships in his classic *Confessions*. Relatively little was written in the Middle Ages about human friendships, though, so keen was the focus on the relationship between man and God.[9] But Albert was keenly aware of its importance and addressed it in his writings—reflecting on Aristotle's notion that the highest level of friendship is based on shared virtues and on Cicero, who wrote "friendship is nothing other than the harmony between things divine and human, with goodwill and love."[10]

One interesting twist to Albert's perspective on friendship is that true friendship, like joy, is *an effect or result* of the virtue of love. Another is that the *self-love* of a virtuous person focuses on the goods of the soul that are best when shared with others, whereas the self-love of a vicious person is focused on one's own material desires, which cannot be shared in kind with others. One more is that even the contemplative needs friends to reach the heights of contemplation, since each individual person stands in some measure "*in potency*," with a potential that can only come to its complete fruition through the interchange of ideas, goodwill, and benevolent deeds with virtuous friends.

Chapter 9

Booted Bishop

For as you have drunk the waters of saving doctrine at
the fount of divine law, in such wise that you carry its
fullness within your breast, while you are possessed of a
true and quick judgment in what pertains to the thing of
God, we entertain the firm hope that by your diligence
you will be able to heal the wounds and repair the ruin of
the aforesaid diocese, which is sadly deficient in things
both spiritual and temporal.

—Pope Alexander IV[1]

The good shepherd lays down his life for his sheep.

—John 10:11

I HAVE an idea for a historical novel. It's late December 1939,
and the United States has just become embroiled in World War
II. The corrupt governor of New York has been impeached, and that
state is in a financial and moral crisis. President Roosevelt, invoking
a new wartime presidential power, decides to appoint the nation's
most brilliant scientist, Albert Einstein himself, as the new governor,
certain that his great mind will be able to restore the state to its glory.
The director of the Institute of Advanced Study in New Jersey urges
Albert to refuse this position, so important is his ongoing work on
a unified field theory for physics. The director reminds him of the
impossibility of pursuing his important theoretical research under the
burdens of such an office, and speaking for his fellow physics professors, begs him to turn down the office.

But Einstein accepts, slipping into the governor's mansion at night without pomp or circumstance and collecting a team of administrators to assist him in the financial rebuilding. He travels around the state in person to exhort public officials to execute their duties of office honorably. He becomes the butt of some jokes, with his accent, his shock of unruly hair, and his ongoing absorption in the world of theoretical physics (always the professor, he continues writing and researching in his spare time). After two years, Einstein has succeeded: New York is fiscally sound, its glory restored. His work accomplished, the world's greatest scientist begs to be given leave of his office and exits with the praise and gratitude of his president.

What do you think? Are you ready to order a copy, or do you think it's a bit too farfetched? Well, let me throw out just one more idea at you, then.

It's early January 1260, and Christendom is embroiled in a battle for its very existence, as Turks and Tatars lead waves of invasions on its eastern borders. The diocese of Ratisbon, Germany, is in financial and moral crisis and its corrupt bishop has been deposed. Pope Alexander IV decides this crisis requires desperate measures and declares that Europe's greatest mind and most brilliant scientist, Albert of Cologne, shall be appointed bishop, in hope that his great mind would restore that diocese to its glory. From his seat at the renowned University of Paris, the general of the Order of Preachers, Blessed Humbert of Romans himself, urges Albert to refuse the position, so important is his ongoing work on the unification of science and theology. The general reminds him of "the impossibility of pursuing a life of contemplation and study amid the cares of such an office," and speaking for his fellow Dominicans, begs him to "send us a reply which will console us and our and your beloved brothers, and will calm our fears."[2]

See where this is going? Albert the Great obeys the pope, slipping into the bishop's mansion at night without pomp or circumstance. He assembles a team of administrators to assist him in the financial rebuilding, and then travels around the diocese in person (by foot, of course) to exhort clergy and public officials to execute their duties honorably. He becomes the butt of some jokes, with his beggar's habit, rough wooden shoes, and ongoing absorption in the worlds of theology and science (about which he continues writing and preaching in his spare time). Two years later, the Diocese of Ratisbon is fiscally sound and its glory restored. The world's greatest scientist begs to be relieved of his administrative duties to return to his life of science. The pope consents, extending Albert his heartfelt thanks.

The second of our little tales of two Alberts—world's greatest scientist to the administrative rescue!—is of course no plot for a novel, but it is a synopsis of historical fact. (And the comparison to a modern governor goes deeper than you might think: in Albert's day the office of bishop carried great civil as well as religious authority. Bishops were like local princes, some even maintaining their own armies to preserve order.)

THE *GREAT* SHEPHERD

Pope Alexander IV was likely taken with Albert's brilliance when the friar lectured at the papal curia on the Gospel of St. John. And word of Albert's successful tenure as provincial, at the helm of a veritable "holy empire" of Dominicans, no doubt carried far. Hugh of St. Cher also likely suggested his great friend to the pope. Yet the Dominican Master General, Blessed Humbert of Romans, was less than pleased at the idea. He wrote to Albert, in very strong language warning him that episcopal appointment could threaten his humility and cause "terrible scandal" within the order.[3] Indeed, he wrote that he would rather hear of Albert's lying in the grave than sitting upon a bishop's throne!

Surely Blessed Humbert knew that Albert's own soul was in little danger, so true was his devotion to God. Further, many Dominicans had become bishops, including the aforementioned Hugh of St. Cher, while doing no damage to their souls or their vows. Indeed, 30

Dominican bishops had attended the Council of Lyons in 1245, 15 years prior.

So why was the leader of the Dominicans so distressed upon hearing of Albert's nomination to the bishopric? For one thing, he thought the timing was bad. The order was finally enjoying a relatively peaceful time after having survived challenges from the secular professors of the University of Paris. Indeed, as we will see in Chapter 15, the pope himself had to settle that dispute, with Albert playing a key role. This was no time for the order to lose so famous and favored a son.

Humbert also wrote that Albert's ascension to the episcopal throne would harm not only the Dominicans but both of the "poor orders." Humbert had engineered a joint encyclical just a few years prior with the Franciscan minister general, urging that the two orders work together for joint survival and preservation of their teaching mission at the University of Paris. He apparently felt that Albert's taking the bishop's crosier would be seen as his acceptance of the ecclesiastical status quo at the peril of the dynamic new orders of mendicant friars. Though he did not name names, Humbert also alluded to others who had accepted esteemed offices only to face great hardships and bear little fruit for their troubles. He suggested too that Albert's move could serve as a justification for others tempted to seek high position for selfish reasons, such as worldly gain and honor and an escape from the rigors of the vow of poverty.

It may also be the case that Humbert had plans for Albert, who had served as a successful provincial, to attain even higher office within their order some day. He was close to resigning as master general due to declining health. Had he been thinking of Albert as a successor?

Unfortunately, we have no record of St. Albert's written response to Blessed Humbert's remarkable letter, but his decision on the matter is history. Though Albert at first politely declined, Pope Alexander IV would have his man: he issued a papal bull announcing Albert's nomination as bishop of Ratisbon on January 5, 1260. In an act of humility Albert chose to obey the will of Peter's successor over Dominic's, and quietly entered the city unannounced on the night of

March 29, 1260. Fittingly, he would spend his first night at the convent of the Church St. Blasé, which was served by the friar-preachers of St. Dominic, and his episcopal installation the next day would take place in the diocese's ancient Roman cathedral, dedicated to St. Peter.

Jesus taught that the Good Shepherd does not abandon his flock, and that he will expend great effort to seek, find, and save even one lost sheep. Albert's predecessor, coincidentally enough named Albert I, Count of Pietengrau, had not been such a shepherd, losing not only his sheep but his own way. After the people wrote him begging for Albert I to be replaced by a worthy successor, Pope Alexander IV deposed Albert I and prescribed for him a period of penitence in a monastery.

The diocese was in a sorry state. Chroniclers note that when Albert arrived at the bishop's palace he found "not a penny in the exchequer, not a drop of wine in the cellar, not a grain of wheat in the granary, and heavy debts to boot."[4] Albert I had borrowed from lenders at high interest and left the diocese in debt to the tune of 486 pounds of gold. Pope Alexander decried the clergy's lax morals, because of which "the name of God is blasphemed on earth . . . religion loses respect with the faithful . . . heretics make us the subject of their bitter mockeries."[5]

This is surely why the pope saw the need for a man of extraordinary intelligence and virtue, a man who could wield the surgeon's knife to cut away dead flesh and the shepherd's staff to scatter the wolves and return God's sheep to the fold. This our Great Shepherd set out to do immediately.

SCIENTIFIC SOWING REAPS REAL REWARDS

When I think of St. Albert's success at renewing his diocese in a mere two years, I can't help but be reminded of the story of Thales, the first of the great philosophers, natural scientists, and sages of ancient Greece. It is said that one year, after repeatedly being chided over the impracticality of his speculation into the workings of nature, Thales used his knowledge of weather patterns and agricultural principles to predict a bumper crop of olives. He then went about and purchased all the local olive presses. When the bumper crop arrived, the supposedly impractical philosopher with his head in the clouds found himself surrounded by money up to his eyeballs.

Perhaps wise Pope Alexander IV knew too how a mind devoted to true *science*, in that broad and ancient sense of a grasping of causes and effects, of a focus on the true nature of things and how they actually work (and in the human realm, on the natural and logical consequences of actions and behaviors), was perfectly suited to diagnosing problems and prescribing their practical cures. He was no academic theologian or spiritual contemplative. From his training as a learned *Bibilici* Albert knew that "faith by itself, if it has no works, is dead."[6] He also knew, as a son of St. Dominic, that the fruits of contemplation are for sharing. Hence, our new bishop wrote to the clergy of his diocese: "We must anticipate the final harvest by works of mercy and, looking forward to eternal riches, sow in time what hereafter we shall bountifully reap. In doing this we must be inspired by a firm hope and great confidence: 'He who soweth sparingly shall reap sparingly; but he who soweth in blessings shall also reap blessings' and shall merit eternal life."[7] Albert traveled throughout the diocese, mostly by foot, meeting with clergy and laity alike, showing a special interest in the monasteries and convents—believing that a renewal of spiritual leadership was an essential first step. Those were especially perilous times for the clergy. Indeed, of the "five wounds of the Church" that had been reported by Pope Innocent IV 15 years prior at the Council of Lyons, a list that included such sorrows as the cruelty of the marauding Tatars in Hungary, the persecutions of Church by the Emperor Frederick, the control of Jerusalem by the Saracens, and the Greek schism, the number one wound had been the immoral behavior of both clergy and laity. Thus, even as he put together and managed a team to fix the diocese's finances, spiritual reform remained Albert's greatest goal.

As Albert traveled his diocese, he displayed the proper pomp when necessary, wearing his bishop's regalia, for example, at public Masses and ceremonies. But in private he continued to live the life a mendicant friar, though he was a Prince of the Church in one of Germany's greatest dioceses. His still wore his crude Dominican footwear as he walked from town to town, earning from detractors the less-than-honorable nickname of *episcopus cum bottis* or *calceatus*—"Bishop Boots."[8]

FAITH HEALER

And when Bishop Albert retired in the evening at some monastery or convent, he continued to share the gift that Mary had promised him decades ago: an unparalleled wisdom about the things of God and nature. Albert wrote at least part of his commentary on the Gospel of St. Luke during this period, finding what time he could in between his travels and administrative duties. An early biographer would call Albert a "second St. Luke," since he too was a man steeped in medicine; he too knew the cure for men's souls.

Albert's writings on St. Luke's gospel give us some glimpses at the depravity of the clergy of his day, boldly denouncing a legion of vices and clerical abuses from luxurious, immoral, and reckless living, to simony (exercising ecclesial powers for profit), to a willful forfeiture of the call to care for souls. And this former provincial of that "German Dominican Empire" would not settle for reform of merely one diocese but forcefully encouraged his episcopal brothers in adjoining dioceses to join him in spiritual reform. Albert, in union with four other German bishops, declared that the censure of any person by one of them would be honored and enforced by all of them. In this way, a person who had defrauded or committed other crimes against the Church could not easily escape punishment merely by moving to the next diocese. Indeed, so strong and so widespread was Albert in his censure that some thought he might never be made a saint (surely he would be spited after death by those whom he had cast in a harsh yet truthful light). Of course, the true saint speaks God's Truth whatever the cost to himself. Of such stuff is sanctity made.

On the temporal side, Albert and his team of administrators ordered that all the episcopal estates, fields, and vineyards be put under full cultivation. It seems Albert's predecessor had been much more interested in sowing the seeds of discord—for example, fanning the flames of conflict between Bohemians and Bavarians within the diocese—than the seeds of grain and grape.

When St. Albert arrived, he tightened the purse strings of his own office; this is in a day when some bishops would arrive at councils with as many as 30 horses in their trains. He eschewed extravagances and gave unneeded furniture from the bishop's palace to the poor. Knowing that charity demands justice, he set up firm regulations and substantial punishments for those who defrauded the Church. For example, he denied Communion and Christian burial to feudal lords and knights who had defrauded the Church of dues and tithes they had collected. Knowing that charity demands mercy as well, he also provided alms in the form of financial aid to many convents, with a preference for those that cared for the poor.

A Prudent Pastor of Souls

When Pope Alexander IV nominated Albert, he called on him to govern the diocese "using the prudence which God has given you."[9] In his *Commentary on the Gospel of St. Luke*, penned or at least completed during his bishopric, Albert would write on the story of Lazarus and the rich man: "Woe to us! for there is no one at the present day to give to the poor; the Pastors of the Church are consecrated, according to the expression of the Prophet, with the best oil, without heeding the sufferings of Joseph, that is, of the poor. They delight in repeating these words of the sinner: 'I have at length found repose; I desire to enjoy my goods alone!'" Albert the philosopher knew that prudence's job is to get the job done by finding the right means to the right ends. We can see one concrete example of how Albert put prudence into practice in the multimodal plan he devised to support the Hospice of St. Catherine, located near Ratisbon's famous bridge, which cared for the sick and the poor. That plan included the following:

- Generously donating from his own resources as bishop
- Preaching incessantly on acts of mercy and almsgiving
- Writing time and again on the needs of the poor and the sick
- Ordering all the priests of his diocese to recommend the project to their parishioners
- Granting an indulgence of 40 days and dispensation from fasting for one year to those who gave generously to the project
- Granting his priests powers to absolve penitents of grave sins, including breaking their vows, mistreating their parents, or missing vowed pilgrimages, if they would give alms to the hospital in proportion to the magnitude of their misdeeds

In another practical move, Albert transferred the feast of the dedication of the basilica of the Benedictine monastery in Prufening from May 12 to the first Sunday after the Ascension. By moving the feast to a Sunday, Albert made it possible for pilgrims to visit the site without having to lose a day's wages. St. Albert would never place mammon or convenience above God, but when he was able to relieve his flock of an impediment to worship, he did not hesitate to do so.

In two years' time, the diocesan treasury was no longer empty. Its debt had been erased. As wise Thales had enriched himself by his science, so too had St. Albert enriched a whole diocese of souls by his. His work done, Albert put Blessed Humbert's fears to rest and resigned. The great son of St. Dominic would return to the fold. And his loyalty to his brothers had not wavered. Indeed, Albert had made sure to introduce to his diocese a new feast: that of St. Dominic.

So successful was Albert in his reforms that despite the brevity of his tenure, some count him among the greatest of all German bishops.

Perhaps his greatest legacy to his successors was his example of leading by example. He modeled both holiness and administrative shrewdness along with hard work and courage. "Bishop Boots" had both literally and figuratively walked his talk. Yet as he progressed through his seventh decade, Albert wanted to return to his core calling, to the study and contemplation that makes possible the fruits to be shared. The pope accepted his resignation. But very soon after his joyous return to the convent and the teaching chair, he would again be called to put his rough boots to the ground and share his wisdom—this time in the hinterlands of Christendom.

GREAT IDEA #9: THE GOOD SHEPHERD

I am the good shepherd; I know my own and my own know me, as the Father knows me and I know the Father; and I lay down my life for the sheep. I have other sheep, that are not of this fold; I must bring them also, and they will heed my voice. So there shall be one flock, one shepherd.

—John 10:14–16

When Jesus declared Himself "the good shepherd," he contrasted Himself with the "hireling" who does not care for his flock and thus flees when the wolf approaches. We have seen that Albert, unlike some bishops of his day, was anything but a hireling. He obediently gave up the pen of the scholar for the staff of the bishop, and he jumped right into the midst of the wolves (both lay and clerical) that were attacking his spiritual sheep.

Albert also sought to reach other sheep far outside the fold of his own diocese. As we will soon see, he did this in many other roles after he resigned his bishopric in Ratisbon. Even in other roles, he would be called on again and again to perform or assist at episcopal functions, such as the consecration of new churches.

Albert was also a shepherd of shepherds. In his years as provincial of the German Dominicans, he helped bring in hundreds of new religious who would reach out around the world to feed Christ's sheep. At the widest level, Albert also most ably assisted Christ's chief shepherd on Earth, the man whose "one flock" encompassed all of Christendom. Time and again Albert heeded the calls of pope after pope to teach at the papal court, to settle disputes between prelates and princes and between warring academic factions, to heal a diocese, and to preach a crusade to defend that largest of all flocks that is the Catholic Church. In his repeated and enduring willingness to set aside his own intellectual and spiritual pursuits to heed his shepherd's call and care for his own flock, Albert truly laid down his life for his sheep. As Providence would have it, by so gladly laying down his life, he built up a truly great one.

In his writings, this great shepherd reaches out even to us in our day, protecting us from the wolves of false doctrines and worldviews, helping us to hear the voice of the one Shepherd who would have us all in His heavenly flock.

Chapter 10

Coped Crusader*

Thus, he relates, how he saw among the Slavonians that
the tribe of the Cumans put ruthlessly to death deformed
children and old people, and boasted gleefully about
their deeds . . . seldom in his written works did Albert
rise to such heights of savage and righteous indignation.

—Thomas Schwertner, O.P.[1]

Truly, I say to you, as you did it to the least of these my
brethren, you did it to me.

—Matthew 25:41

DURING his life Albert was a "crusader" according to two senses
of the word "crusade." The first embodies definition number
three in my *American Heritage Dictionary*, specifically, a "vigorous
movement for a cause." The second pertains directly to definition
number one, that is, "any of the military expeditions undertaken by

---

*The *cope* (also called *cape*) was a long liturgical vestment that was open in front and held
together by an ornamented clasp called a *morse*. As a Dominican friar, Albert wore the white,
coarse, woolen habit of his order. During the time he served as bishop, he wore the appropriate
liturgical vestments for that role. His cope bore a golden cross on the front and on the back. His
rochet, a white ceremonial garment worn by bishops, had no lace but featured five red stripes,
representing the five wounds of Christ. His bishop's hat or *miter* was not excessively tall and
was simply adorned, and his *crosier* or bishop's staff was plain and made of wood, but for an
ivory crook bearing a carving of the Archangel Gabriel leaning toward Albert's great object
of devotion, the Holy Virgin Mary. Adapted in part from S. M. Albert, O.P., *Albert the Great*
(Oxford: Blackfriars Publications, 1948), 44.

European Christians in the 11th, 12th, and 13th centuries to recover the Holy Land from the Moslems." Let's look at them both now.

A MEDIEVAL CULTURE OF DEATH

As for the first "crusade," we might also call it an apostolic mission. Sometime after January in the year 1256, Pope Alexander IV, a few years before he would call Albert to his bishopric in Ratisbon, sent Albert and a small group of his peers to the far reaches of the frontier lands of Poland, Prussia, and Livonia in the office of a papal legate. These were the lands in which Albert's Dominican forbears St. Hyacinth and his Brother Ceslaus brought so many souls to Christ yet repeated invasions from Tatars and Mongols had wreaked havoc and restored many barbarous laws and brutal pagan customs.

Though the trip is only sparsely documented, one of the documents that mentions it is Albert's own *Politics*. And indeed, even if the whole episode were spurious, its lesson is amazingly relevant to our day as it portrays a barbaric "culture of death" so eerily similar to our own. Commenting on that age in his biography of St. Albert, Father Sighart notes that "no one has rights over his fellow-creature as though he were no more than a mere brute—such crimes ought naturally to excite horror."[2]

All right, what were these horrible crimes? They slaughtered children born with deformities, since they could not bear arms or serve their parents or their state; they determined the number of children each family could rear; they euthanized the elderly who were unfit for labor or service. All this they did without a second thought (Albert reported that they would proudly point out the graves of their own parents they had massacred). Albert was outraged that they still dared to call themselves Christians.

Indeed, can you imagine the anger and sadness in the heart of a man so sensitive to human dignity, so profoundly aware of how man is made in God's image? Yet Albert trusted in the power of God to change men's souls, and he preached with apostolic zeal and love to effect a reversion to Christ. We have little evidence of the outcome of Albert's mission, but an early biographer tells that Albert was consoled by the salvation of many souls by the fact that German Dominican missionary volunteers soon after increased in their numbers, and, later, by a second call to preach at the far-off borders of Christian Europe.

PREACHER OF THE CROSS FOR THE DELIVERANCE OF THE HOLY PLACES

Many a successor of St. Peter would call upon Albert's talents during his long life. Not long after fulfilling Alexander IV's request to renew the Diocese of Ratisbon, while Albert was once again enjoying academic and religious life with his Dominican brothers in Cologne, "with the joy of a bird that escapes from his fowler's net,"[3] as Sighart so felicitously phrases it, another great pontiff was preparing to net again our great saint.

Pope Urban IV was no stranger to the Holy Land, having been patriarch of Jerusalem prior to his election as pope in 1261. He was acutely aware of the threat to all of Christendom should Islam continue in its march through the West unchecked. Jerusalem, Palestine, North Africa, and even Christian Constantinople were harassed by the Moslems. Seven crusades from 1096 to 1254 had failed to return the Holy Land to Christian hands. This new pope believed it was time to fire Christian swords and Christian hearts for another valiant attempt to regain what had been lost in the Holy Land and to protect what could be lost in Europe.

Much of Christian Europe, however, was embroiled in strife and turmoil of its own. Poland and Hungary faced Tatar invasions, Spain was at war with the Moors, Prussia and Lithuania suffered pagan invasions, and England faced internal discord. It would fall to France, Italy, and Germany to take up the Cross and regain the lands of Palestine, and as of February 13, 1263, it would fall to St. Albert and his copapal legate, the bold and powerful Franciscan preacher Berthold of Ratisbon, to preach the crusade to Germany and Bohemia.

Their task was to win men and money to the papal cause. Money they raised partly through alms, for which were provided certain indulgences (some argue that this may have given rise to the false notion that indulgences were "sold"[4]). They also possessed the power to commute, for a sliding fee, the vows of men who had committed themselves to fight in the Crusade, and later, for whatever reasons, found that they could not or would not go. Those funds too went toward the expenses of the Crusade.

So, well into his sixties, St. Albert crisscrossed throughout Germany for over a year, preaching the crusade and performing many of the other acts for which he was called great—studying, writing, hearing confessions, visiting convents, settling disputes, and sundry other deeds. Father Schwertner wrote in 1932 that up to that moment no documents bearing upon Albert's activities as a preacher of the Crusade had been found. Neither do I find mention of any in Father Weisheipl's brief biography of 1980 or in Resnick and Kitchell's annotated bibliography of Albertine writings from 1900 to 2000. We are left, therefore, only with conjecture about Albert's words and deeds bearing directly on this Crusade.

From what we know about Albert and from the patchwork of other reported deeds carried out in various German cities during this timeframe, it is possible to put together in a general way St. Albert's game plan. As a scientist and a philosopher, Albert was aware of the various classes and kinds of causes required to bring about specific effects. We lack documentation of the most proximate or immediate causes that Albert used to persuade the German people to join the Crusade to the Holy Land—we don't know the words he used to persuade them—but we can see from Albert's other practical actions, such as his efforts to provide for the Hospital of St. Catherine while bishop, that he was one to attack problems from many angles, setting into play many different kinds and levels of causal factors to bring about his desired effects.

We know for a fact that Pope Urban IV gave Albert extraordinary powers to grant indulgences to those who gave alms for the Crusades (as well as for other worthy projects and pious practices). Also, many of Albert's surviving sermons date from this period, and although they do not include specific exhortations to take up the Cross in Crusade, we can see how they most certainly fit into a grand plan to fire up men's hearts for the Gospel—and inspire them to defend Holy Mother Church and European Christendom.

From Sword and Sheath to Laurel Wreath

Most of us tend to do best the things we most enjoy, the activities that best suit our temperaments, inclinations, and talents. One key to St. Albert's true greatness is that he did his best at *whatever activities Providence placed in his way*. As the scholar had become the administrator, now did the peacemaker become war recruiter. St. Albert knew that the gift of wisdom, the beatitude of peacemaking, and the fruit of peace all flowed from the infusion of the theological virtue of *charity*. He knew as well that from that the moral virtue of *justice* flowed the beatitude of hungering for righteousness, that a proper vengeance was a virtue related to justice, and that some wars were therefore just. He knew that Jerusalem had been justly won back in the First Crusade, before being lost again. He knew as well of the danger to the Church and to all of European Christendom, that font of God's charity, from the Muslim threat in the East. This is how this man of wisdom and charity could rouse his brothers to arms.

It was certainly not for want of his efforts that the Crusade languished, that Jerusalem was never recovered. The last document bearing Albert's name as *Praedicator Crucis*, Preacher of the Cross for the Crusade, was signed on August 25, 1264. Less than six weeks later, Urban IV passed away. His successor, Clement IV, held different priorities, and was faced with intensified strife and turmoil among the various nations of Europe. So the eighth and last great Crusade would not commence for another six years.

Finally, Albert would have the leisure to read, pray, think, write, and preach until the end of his days on Earth. He retired first to the priory of Wurzburg, where his now full-grown brother Henry was prior and his dear friend Ulric von Strasbourg resided. Later, he would live for a time at the priory of Strasbourg, and from 1271 until his death in 1280, St. Albert of Cologne found himself back home in the convent of Cologne. But the great man would still sally forth from the convent walls at times, to cry peace (and achieve it) among both figuratively and literally warring parties (the stuff of our next chapter) and, at times, to draw his own figurative sword in defense of his intellectual and spiritual brothers of the mendicant orders and in defense of his intellectual and spiritual son, St. Thomas Aquinas himself.

GREAT IDEA #10: THE VIRTUE *AND* *GIFT* OF FORTITUDE

Fortitude is the virtue that overcomes obstacles to the good. It fights or endures to acquire arduous or difficult goals. Under the guidance of reason, it is the virtue that moderates our "irascible appetite," most often by firing up our "ire" to face fearsome or painful events or circumstances. Fortitude derives from the Latin word *fortis,* meaning "strength," and a person who has trained himself by repeated practice to possess the virtue of fortitude will display that strength whether the difficulties he faces are physical, intellectual, or spiritual ones.

We have seen and will continue to see how St. Albert prevailed as a pillar of strength and fortitude in body, mind, and soul. But there is more to fortitude than hard-won natural virtue. As Isaiah had told us,[5] fortitude is also among the gifts of the Holy Spirit, and with this perfection of fortitude St. Albert was also abundantly blessed. Natural virtues are the oars with which we row ourselves toward the good. The gifts of the Holy Spirit are the wind in our sails that propels us toward the highest Good of all. St. Albert accepted that gift of fortitude, which gave him confidence and assurance so that even when his physical strength and intellectual prowess declined, he would prevail to the end, patiently and joyfully awaiting the renewed and glorified strength of eternal life.

Chapter 11
Pontifical Peacemaker

Albert, who in his lifetime labored strenuously and
successfully for peace between princes and peoples and
individual men, is put before us now as the perfect model
of peace . . . He presented a living image of his Master,
whom Scripture calls "the Prince of Peace."

—Pope Pius XI[1]

You should make your heart like your neighbor's heart,
so that when he is happy you are happy, and you grieve
with him when he is grieving.

—St. Albert the Great[2]

THE 13th century was a tumultuous time for the people of the
developing Germanic city-states. Bishops behaved like temporal princes, often fighting with each other, the nobility, and the
common people to increase their wealth and power. Typically the
combatants showed few signs of Christian charity. And along with
these deadly sins of pride and avarice, their fellow travelers of wrath,
envy, and spiritual sloth were often to be found.

How ironic, and yet how fitting, it was that the man called in to
mediate these squabbles among the wealthy and worldly was one
who had traded his noble birthright for a beggar's robe, that the arbiter extraordinaire of practical political conflicts was a scholar most at
home when surrounded by ancient texts, and that those who rejected
authority for their own gain would be faced down by a man who held
inviolate his vows of poverty and obedience.

St. Paul said we must die to ourselves and let Christ live through us. So many times did St. Albert heed this call, setting aside his desires to read, study, teach, and write in peace when he was called into action to bring peace instead to unruly people, often disputing about things most petty. Albert, of course, saw Christ in each of them, and never rejected his calling as peacemaker, striving to settle matters as fairly as humanly possible while imploring a heavenly forgiveness from all parties. One of many aphorisms attributed to Albert goes as follows: "To forgive those who have injured us in our body, our reputation, our goods, is more advantageous to us than to cross the seas to go to venerate the Sepulchre of our Lord."[3] Albert knew that from God's loving charity flows the gift of wisdom, from which in turn come the beatitude of peacemaking and the fruit of peace itself. Let's examine a few examples then of the ways in which our scientist-saint transformed discord and conflict into harmony and peace.

ARCHBISHOPS AND ARCHRIVALS

In the year 1250, during the time of Albert's appointment as regent at the new *Studium Generale* in Cologne, around the time that he helped draft the system of study for his Dominican order, and years before Albert's served as provincial and later bishop, it seems that Archbishop Conrad of Hochstaden and the citizens of Albert's own Cologne were not exactly modeling Christian charity. In fact, bitter strife, struggle, and even military engagement were afoot. Wealthy merchants had decided to free themselves from the archbishop's jurisdiction and refused to recognize his authority, even though, as Sighart relates, "next to the Emperor, he was the most powerful and the first Prince of the State."[4]

Archbishop Conrad had retaliated by levying a heavy tax (remember, at that time bishops had considerable temporal powers, too) on previously exempt merchandise. He established a customs house at Nuess, a small town across the Rhine from Cologne, and the citizens responded in turn by smuggling goods to avoid the tolls. Further, he disregarded the town's exclusive privilege to mint money by coining his own. The municipal leaders sought out Conrad at the episcopal palace to voice their grievances. Conrad took little truck with their complaints, refused to yield or compromise, and left for his fortress at Andernach, where he prepared for war.

During the Lenten season in 1251 the archbishop sailed down the Rhine in his warships, landed at Nuess, that small town across the river, and besieged Cologne with armed troops. He was not pleased to see that the citizens were not prepared to fight in open battle but rather had settled in to endure a siege. At the prompting of an overly optimistic military engineer, he sent a boat loaded with "Greek fire"—a deadly mixture of combustible liquids—down the Rhine to destroy a merchant fleet, but that boat itself was the only vessel that went up in smoke.[5]

His siege was unsuccessful, leaving the disputing parties at an impasse, and Archbishop Conrad eventually appointed two Dominicans to arbitrate the peace. One was Cardinal Hugo of St. Sabina (also known as Hugh of St. Cher before becoming Cardinal of St. Sabina in 1244), a papal legate, and the other was Cologne's own Brother Albert. Hugo, however, was traveling at the time, and so Albert negotiated the peace singlehandedly. It was a masterpiece of diplomatic compromise. The archbishop would be allowed two mintings of coins, his new taxes were lifted, the citizens were required to cease smuggling in goods to avoid taxes, and a general peace and amnesty was to commence. The archbishop would also promise to defend the citizens, both Christian and Jew, while the citizens would acknowledge his traditional office and rights as bishop and prince.

Remember that these were times that recalled Christ's wounds, and one of the festering open wounds of the day was the rampant vice of both clergy and the laity. It was not long, therefore, before the Albertine peace was rent asunder. Proud Archbishop Conrad had never fully relinquished his designs for greater power and apparently felt inordinately penalized by the settled peace. For the next several years he wrangled with the merchants, breeding resentment through various legalistic quibblings and rendering decisions to their disadvantage. Though details are sparse, while Albert was in Anagni, Italy, in 1256, the archbishop again assembled armed forces to attack the citizens of Cologne, ostensibly in retaliation for an assault upon the person of a canon lawyer.

Conrad himself mounted a warhorse to lead the attack, which took place in a field near the village of Frechen. But he was defeated in a bloody battle, and his forces were scattered by an army of citizens led by one Thierry of Falkenberg. Albert again was called in, presiding over a commission to negotiate a new peace, carefully and justly weighing the claims and counterclaims of each of the warring parties. That peace eventually gave way to further (though lesser) conflicts, and Albert intervened with some success for a third time in 1260. Shortly after that, the contentious Archbishop Conrad went to his grave.

Albert spent the early 1260s in Ratisbon as its bishop. Soon after followed his preaching of the Crusade throughout Germany. From 1264 to 1267 he would call home the Dominican cloister of Wurzburg, where his own brother Henry resided. Here, surely contented in his most natural role, he lectured in theology and wrote commentaries on the metaphysical and logical writings of Aristotle. In 1265 he was pulled again from his lecture hall when Pope Clement IV asked him to help mediate a conflict between the bishop of Strasbourg and the city's burghers, who had challenged his traditional episcopal powers (a recurring theme in 13th-century Germany) and ransacked churches and monasteries. After placing his signature first on the treaty, Albert returned to his quiet life.

By 1271 Albert was back in Cologne and perhaps anticipating a peaceful semiretirement of prayer and study. But the new archbishop, Engelbert, another warlike prince in the spirit of Archbishop Conrad, found himself in disagreement with the city's citizens—as evidenced by the fact that Count William of Julich had imprisoned him in the Castle of Nideggen for over three years! The details on the conflict are sparse, but we can safely assume that they involved common themes of ecclesiastical versus municipal authority, as well as commercial and financial issues.

By the time Albert returned, the count had been excommunicated and the city placed under papal interdict.[6] That meant that the count and the citizens were not entitled to the ministrations of the Church, that is, to public worship in the Mass or to the Sacraments. Both temporal and spiritual anarchy were at hand when the Dominican Master General John of Vercelli, the sixth in the history of their order, asked the universally respected Albert to wade in. Before long, the great peacemaker arranged to have the papal interdict removed, provided that the people once more recognized the archbishop's rightful authority and with the promise that the archbishop would not seek vengeance on the city or the count but rather "that as a father he will suffer the insult to be forgotten."[7]

In the years between those two incidents in Cologne, Albert was called on to settle other disputes, besides the tumultuous events in Strasbourg. For instance, in 1264 he effected a settlement between the collegiate Church of St. John and a nobleman named Gottfried of Hohenlohe regarding the rights of college provosts. The next year he was called in to settle a similar dispute. And once, after a bitter and contentious feud erupted between the secular academics of the University of Paris and the mendicant orders of St. Francis and St. Dominic, Pope Alexander IV called St. Albert to his court at Anagni for help in settling the dispute. We'll look at Albert's great victory in this affair in Chapter 15.

An interesting civil case requiring Albert's artful arbitration, involving a property dispute, occurred in 1265. One Wegenheim of Wurzburg had built stables so close to the custom house that it blocked the lighting of the building. What better man to settle even such a sundry conflict than the great friar who knew all the knowledge there was to know? Another documented case involves Albert's brokering of a peace between the Knights of St. John in Wurzburgand and the knight Marquard.

Though the dates and details of some of these disputes are lost to time, we know that Albert was so often called on to resolve them and that at least in the short run, his resolutions were well-received by the disputing parties.

AND PEACE BE WITH THEM, TOO

We can speculate as to why St. Albert was so repeatedly cast in the role of the peacemaker. Even in a time when so many people's vision of justice was clouded by self-interest, disputing parties seemed to be able to recognize—and respect—Albert's deep wisdom and justice. They wanted their cases decided by the "man who knew everything"—and who was holy, humble, and honest to boot. For Albert's part, surely his skill at understanding the natures of things (and people), combined with his long and broad experience in matters both temporal and spiritual, served him well as a diplomat and as an architect of compromise between the Church and the world.

It is not through any particular faults or inadequacies in Albert's resolutions that some of his brokered treaties failed; for this we must blame the fallen nature of man, who must learn lessons of righteousness again and again and again. We saw that Albert fervently preached forgiveness, and that he himself forgave, remaining ever willing to sally forth from the sweet joys of his scholarly and spiritual pursuits to come to the aid of his order, his pontiff, and his neighbors, to do whatever good works God asked of him. The thinker was never above dirtying his hands (but never his soul) when called upon as a doer.

AND THE GREATEST OF THESE IS LOVE

In parts I and II we looked at ways in which St. Albert, in his many moral and intellectual virtues and in the roles he played, was a great *thinker* and great *doer*. Of course, there is a higher set of virtues yet, and with them come yet higher roles. These are the stuff of part III: the theological virtues, of which the greatest is love.[8] Onward we go then, to look at how Albert's greatness was revealed in his love.

GREAT IDEA #11: PEACE

There can be no true peace except where the appetite is
directed to what is truly good. Hence true peace is only
in good men and about good things.

—St. Thomas Aquinas[9]

Albert was a consummate peacemaker among men because peace,
like joy, is an effect that flows from charity, an infused virtue with
which Albert was abundantly blessed. Peace is a concordance or harmony of desires among persons. When those persons' desires are not
fully just and their thoughts are not focused on good and honorable
ends, peace will not last long. We have seen this play out in the transient effects of some of St. Albert's wise arbitrations. He knew well
that true peace was only possible among good men, and that is why
his greatest peacemaking efforts were performed not in the settlement of sundry disputes but through his teaching and preaching: by
making men good.

There is also a peace that we desire within our own souls. This
peace is a calmness or tranquility born of a harmonious order within
our own desires. As a young man Albert lacked such inner peace until
he was able to envision harmony between his desire for knowledge
and his desire for sanctity; harmony that was later actualized in the
life of the scientist-saint.

If true peace is only found among good men focused on good
things, we would do well to imagine the depth of peace within the
soul of a great man focused on the highest things. We would do even
better actively to seek such harmony within our own souls and with
our own neighbors, taking that great man as our model. What things
might we, aided by the model and the intercession of St. Albert, do
today to foster peace with someone with whom we have quarreled, or
within our own restless souls?

PART III

LOVER

Chapter 12

Mary's Minstrel

Oh, how sweet is Mary's image! See, what care art-
ists take to make it surpass in beauty those of other
saints. See how solicitous are the faithful to show it due
veneration. Churches are adorned with her pictures that
our thoughts may dwell devoutly on her. In heaven we
shall behold not her image in marble or on canvas, but
her own most beautiful soul and body. We shall gaze on
her sweet countenance, and its beauty shall ravish us
throughout eternity.

—St. Albert the Great[1]

If a maiden, her arms laden with beautiful flowers, would
beckon us to her side, how willingly would we follow
the summons; if a queen bade us approach, we would
probably do so with some hesitation. But behold, the
Queen of the virgins, the Queen of queens calls us, and
we heed not her words. Strange inconsistency!

—St. Albert the Great[2]

THE low book case that adjoins my desk and runs along the length
of a wall in our study is adorned with decorations that tell a
little of our family story. Like Albert, I'm a devotee of the wisdom
of Greece and Rome, so it holds some of my "ancient" treasures—a
bust of the Greek god Poseidon, another of Athena, a marble pen-
holder with five pens that look like different styles of ancient Greek
columns, a replica of a Roman centurion's helmet, massive red plume

and all, an actual Roman coin from the fourth century AD, a copper Grecian urn bearing painted scenes form Homer's *Iliad*, and a pure white statue of a young Augustus Caesar. These were the decorations I acquired before my return to the Church six years ago.

Since that time new ornaments have accrued. In the corner now are three crosses. One of them, a gift from my father, also bears the image of St. Gerard of Majella (Mom miscarried five times before I was born, which is why I bear the middle name of that patron saint of childbirth). The other two are crucifixes that once sat in places of great honor: upon Mom's and Dad's caskets. You will also find a beautiful statue of a man in the Dominican garb of black and white, a replica of a church resting on an open book in his left hand, depicting how his great writings upheld and revealed the glories of the Church, an emblem of the sun on his chest, representing how the light of his wisdom has illuminated our understanding, and a golden aureole over his head, clear symbol of his saintliness—yes, it is Albert's stellar student, the Angelic Doctor, St. Thomas Aquinas.

My wife, Kathy, has keepsakes, too. There's a battered old Bible of her mother's, upon which sits a two-inch-long children's book containing one verse from every book of the Bible. Next to the aforementioned statue of Augustus Caesar is a large metal crucifix, standing on a base, from a Michigan church now torn down. Augustus's extended right finger points right up to the corpus, which is why we call this the "Mark 12:18" or the "Render unto Caesar" arrangement, as if Caesar himself is declaring by his gesture, "Render unto me what is mine, and unto Him what is His!"

One study wall is adorned with *L'Innocence*, that famous 18th-century painting of Mary holding baby Jesus and a baby lamb. The surface of my desk includes a plaque of a Polish icon of Mary and the child Jesus, and also a very small keepsake box with the Mother and Child motif. Nearly new is a statue of golden color of Our Lady of Manaog, a gift from my son freshly home from the Philippines.

Then there's the latest adornment, a gift from my wife just a few days ago: an antique statue of Mary, Queen of Heaven. Her robe and veil match the yellow and gold of the study walls, set off by the stunningly calm and beautiful sky blue of her cape. Her arms are held down with her palms facing forward, extending to us God's bounteous graces. Her foot rests upon the head of a serpent, ready to crush it.

The artist has crafted the statue's features with the greatest of care, surely to depict his own conception of heavenly perfection, the "sweetest" possible image, "surpassing in beauty." Let this newest acquisition of mine serve as our focal point as we explore St. Albert's love and devotion to the Blessed Mother, and the beautiful Marian images and doctrines that he has crafted for us.

MARY'S MERITS

All biographers highlight the great role the Blessed Virgin Mary played in Albert's life and in his writings. She abounds in the legends, too. It was she who told him to join the Dominicans and she who responded to his request for great knowledge that would not threaten his faith. During his youth in Padua, Albert spent hours before her image in a Dominican church and later wrote that she inspired him with courage to study and seek truth.

In later and quieter times he would compose and sing hymns to her as he strolled and prayed in his garden. Albert would write about Mary many different times within many different books and sermons throughout his lifetime, but his most extensive and famous book was his *Mariale* or *230 Questions Concerning the Virgin Mary*. It is believed to be one of his earliest works. Within its pages, Albert specifically addresses a full 90 questions to Mary's virtues and graces. So deep is his fascination and devotion that even her height, the cast of her complexion, and the color of her hair and eyes are subjects of consideration.

Always such a true Dominican, a thinker and a lover, Albert in the *Mariale* masterfully employs the evidence-based style of the Aristotelian logician, complete with the meticulous and systematic question-and-answer format of the scholastic theologian, yet delivers lines of lyrical delight that would recall a long-past Homer or perhaps suggest a not-yet-born Shakespeare. A classical Homeric formula for the break of day, for instance, is "*rhododactylos Eos*" or "rosy-fingered dawn." Albert compares the Virgin to Eos's Latin equivalent, *aurora*, or in English, dawn. Solomon asks, "Who is this that looks forth like the dawn, fair as the moon, bright as the sun?"[3] Albert answers that the dawn is Mary. The night is her eternal predestination, and she is the dawn that ushers in the full and perfect light of the Son. She is "the dawn of all grace unto our glory—the dawn rising in the fullness of grace and yet growing even into the perfection of day."[4]

Albert details how Mary was blessed with and embodies all the virtues and graces, including the intellectual and cardinal and theological virtues, the 7 gifts of the Holy Spirit, the 8 beatitudes, and the 12 fruits of the Holy Spirit. (We cover many of these virtues and graces in the Great Ideas boxes within this book, with a special emphasis on how St. Albert displayed them.) Albert tells us that not only does Mary perfectly embody the virtues, but she also fervently desires to share them with us through her intercession and mediation.

We saw in Chapter 4 how Albert the philosopher was blessed at birth with many natural virtues and gifted by God with an abundance of theological virtue—all ordered toward the evangelical purpose for which God made him. He loved the virtues and endeavored to understand them more deeply, and to expound them more clearly for our benefit. As Albert saw, though, Mary's fullness of all grace flowed from an even higher honor bestowed by God, one unique in all the universe and for all eternity, and was ordered toward the highest of God's purposes. Mary then, through God's overflowing graces, was the literal *embodiment* of virtue, much in the way that her *fiat*, that great "yes" to God at the Annunciation, allowed for the literal embodiment or *incarnation* of the divine Source all of grace and virtue. For this reason, "the person of the Blessed Virgin is the most excellent under God, and above every other creature the most worthy of all creatures."[5]

THE MATERNITY OF MARY

Albert tells us that when the Archangel Gabriel addressed Mary as "full of grace," he essentially gave her a new name, a name that no other creature in the universe could claim, and that there was an extremely important reason for this. Central to Albert's Mariology is her divine maternity, her predestined honor to be the bearer of God incarnate. For an even higher grace than being the son of God by adoption is to be the Mother of God by nature. Indeed, ever the Aristotelian philosopher, he notes that to be "the Mother of God by nature though not God" is a mean between "being the Son of God by nature and truly God, and being the Son God by adoption and not God." The only state higher for Mary would be divinity itself. There, of course, Albert never goes. He knew only too well the difference between the created and the Creator, even when considering his most beloved and blessed creature.

In the *Mariale* and in his *Commentary on St. Luke's Gospel,* St. Albert pores over the event of the Annunciation with the greatest of care, exploring every detail of its rich meaning. He ponders whether it was necessary that an archangel be sent to the Virgin, under what form the Angel appeared, whether it wore clothing and of what type, what time of day or night it occurred, in which city and why.

In his investigation of these seemingly minute details, Albert provides us with truly sublime and profound essential principles. For example, echoing and refining the Marian doctrines of St. Bernard from the previous century, he infers that at the same time the Divine Wisdom predestined the Incarnation of Christ, so too was Mary predestined to divine maternity. This implies that both human history as a whole, and Mary's history in particular, prepared for the realization of his salvific plan.

Like the early Church Fathers before him, Albert loved to search the pages of the Old Testament to find prophecies, as well as *types* or prefigurements of Mary and her maternity. St. Albert borrows from and builds on the insights of St. Jerome, for example, in his

explications on prophecies and types in the texts of Isaiah and Jeremiah. Consider Isaiah 11:1: "There shall come forth a shoot from the
stump of Jesse, and a branch shall grow out of his roots." This shoot,
notes St. Albert, represents Mary as Mother of God. That shoots are
"long and straight, upright and solid, graceful and flexible—here are
all the symbols of the graces of Mary."[6] The branch, of course, is
Christ, who in the very next verse is rested upon by the Holy Spirit,
receiving all of his gifts. St. Albert notes as well in his *Commentary
on St. Luke* that "the virginal process in which the stalk gives birth to
the flower recalls the virginal birth."[7]

The prophet Jeremiah (31:22) proclaims, "For the Lord has created
a new thing on the earth: a woman protects a man." For St. Albert, the
glorious "new" thing would be the union of divinity with humanity
in this birth, since, of course, the union of soul and body within man
is nothing new at all. Some English translations use the word "com-
pass" instead of "protects"; St. Albert used Jerome's Latin translation
of "*circumdabit*," to encircle or enclose, noting the wondrous mystery that though Christ in his divinity is infinite and boundless, he
would be enclosed within the confines of his earthly mother's womb.

St. Albert believed that over the course of time the scriptural images
of Mary become progressively clearer. Indeed, we may observe a
parallel process in the history of the Church, in which the understanding of Marian doctrines has grown progressively clearer, culminating
in the official dogmatic proclamations of the Immaculate Conception
and the Assumption of Mary, centuries after Albert's time.

The *Catechism of the Catholic Church* confirms Mary's predestination (paragraph 488) and her prefiguration in the Old Testament,
through many holy women who prepared her way, such as Sarah,
Hannah, Deborah, Ruth, Judith, Esther, and many others. "Against all
human expectation God chooses those who were considered powerless
and weak to show forth their faithfulness to his promise" (489). Or as
St. Albert wrote in his *Commentary on St. Luke*, "Truly, only the Fortitude of God could unite the most lowly and the most exalted, the first
and the last, God and man in the womb of Mary the Mother of God."[8]

St. Albert compared Mary to Noah's ark, the tabernacle of Moses, the Temple, the house and throne of Solomon, the burning bush of Moses, the sapphire throne above the firmament, the tree reaching up to Heaven, the altar of Gideon, the little fountain growing into a river; he saw expressions of Mary in the beautiful virgin Esther, the spouse Rebecca, Rachel, the widow Judith, Abraham's wife Sara, and Mary's own cousin Elizabeth, mother of John the Baptist. Father Genevois counts 137 figures of Mary cited in Albert's many works.[9] Here's one sample: in answer to the 19th question of the *Mariale*, "Did the Blessed Virgin possess a perfect knowledge of the seven liberal arts?" we read, "It seems to me that she did, for it is written, 'Wisdom hath built herself a house, she hath hewn her out seven pillars' (Prov. Ix.1). This house is the Blessed Virgin; the seven pillars are the seven liberal arts. Mary was, then, endowed with a perfect knowledge of them."[10] St. Albert himself did not propound the doctrine of the Immaculate Conception, erroneously thinking, as did St. Bernard before him, that it would have required Mary's mother St. Ann to have been a virgin mother herself. (Not even great Albert was all-knowing!) Still, two centuries before the Feast of the Immaculate Conception was instituted in 1476, and six centuries before its formal proclamation as dogma in 1854, Albert was convinced of Mary's "negative sanctity" or absence of sin as a fitting prerequisite for her holy maternity.

This calls to my mind the stages of growth in the love of God described by St. Thomas. The beginner in charity fights against sin, the person growing in charity builds virtue, and those highest in charity seek only God. But in Mary, says Albert, from the beginning there was no sin and *all* virtues, including the highest of charity, infused in her soul. Charity desires union with God, and that Mary achieved like no other.

The Merry Mariologist

St. Albert's devotion to Mary prompted him to devote more written words to her than any other writer of the Middle Ages, many of the phrases waxing poignantly eloquent. He also advanced the sacred science of Mariology in his classic Albertine manner of grand synthesis, gathering and honing truths from far and wide—from the logical and dialectical methods of the Aristotelians, to the Church Fathers, to recent theologians such as St. Bernard of Clairvaux and Peter Lombard, to his own incredible depth of knowledge of Sacred Scripture. When on November 1, 1950, nearly 700 years after Albert's death, Pope Pius XII defined the dogma of the Assumption of Mary, he wrote, "When, during the Middle Ages, scholastic theology was especially flourishing, St. Albert the Great, who to establish this teaching had gathered together many proofs from Sacred Scripture, from the statements of older writers, and finally from the liturgy and from what is known as theological reasoning, concluded in this way: 'From these proofs and authorities and from many others, it is manifest that the most blessed Mother of God has been assumed above the choirs of angels. And this we believe in every way to be true.'"[11] When I read of Albert the Great's devotion to the Virgin Mary, I can't help but think of a man from our time whom some now call great. Karol Josef Wojtyla was also a profound philosopher and theologian with a special devotion to God's holy mother. A professor and preacher, he traveled extensively and wore many hats, including the hat of pontiff, of course, during his reign as Pope John Paul II. That Mary brought each of them joy and consolation, this is clear. For scientist-theologians who see how creation points us to God, what greater source of contemplative joy than the most blessed of all of His creatures?

What a glorious image it is: St. Albert the Great, the brilliant man of science, the mathematician, the learned doctor and university professor, the provincial of an order, the bishop of a diocese, the Aristotelian logician, the man of his generation, strolling through the garden of the Convent of Cologne, singing hymns to Blessed Mary. Biographers note that Albert never mentions the Virgin Mary without a holy epithet: Blessed Virgin, Mother of God, Star of the Seas, and so on. In referring to her as the Star of the Sea, he states that even her name declares it: "For it is Mary (*Maria*), because, as in the sea (*mare*), there is gathered together all the waters, so in Mary is there gathered together all graces."[12] No wonder he has been called the "Preeminent Mariologist" (*Praestantissimus Mariologus*)[13] and "Mary's Private Secretary."[14]

All who share the same mother and father are of course brothers and sisters. As St. Albert's heart burned with the love of God's charity for the Mother of God, so too did he burn to care for the spiritual needs of his sisters in Christ who lived in his own day. In the next chapter we shall see how this great man of reason and stern manly virtues poured forth his heart to foster the growth of devout groups of religious women in his day.

GREAT IDEA #12: THE VIRTUE OF PIETY

St. Albert was known far and wide for his justice in settling disputes among warring parties and for setting things right between man and God in the confessional. But Albert knew that justice is not only a matter of imposing fair conditions upon others but also a matter of building virtue within one's own soul. He knew from Aristotle that the virtue of justice requires that we render to others their rightful due through *repeated acts of the will*. The virtue of justice can be further examined and perfected through the development of related virtues that direct our just acts toward certain particular objects, such as specific classes of individuals, and the virtue of *piety* is one of that number.

Piety or *filial respect* is the virtue through which we render our rightful due to our kindred, especially our parents, and to our country. It appears that Albert's own parents died early in his life, but one clear example of Albert's piety is the homage and service we have seen him bestow on behalf of his heavenly mother, Mary. As for the care and respect for his country and his fellow citizens, we saw how Albert "of Cologne" came to shepherd the people of Ratisbon as well, and indeed how he led a veritable holy Germanic empire as a provincial of his order. Throughout his career he also showed the highest of deference and respect to a very special father: the pope himself.

The virtue of piety also touches, in its highest form of excellence, the worship of God the Father. Certainly Albert's fervent love and respect for the Maternity of Mary was only exceeded by his all-consuming love of charity for the Paternity of God.

Chapter 13

Lady Lover

The fire of Divine love which the disciples of St. Francis and St. Dominic spread abroad by their preaching and holy example, inflamed not only a multitude of men in Germany, who consecrated themselves to God's Service, but a great number of women who aspired to the same sacrifices.

—Joachim Sighart[1]

Chevalier Arnold, minister of the Bishop of Osnabruck, sought out the illustrious servant of God, Albert, in order that he might found, by his authority and wisdom, a Convent of women, according to the Rule and with the habit of St. Dominic. Albert consented; and when he learnt how this pious community was prepared to run after the sweets of the Spouse, he praised God with all the powers of his soul.

—Rodolph of Nijmegen[2]

IN 1995 Pope John Paul II addressed a letter to the women of the world on the occasion of the Fourth World Conference on Women in Beijing, China. His letter was full of thanks to women, of honor and respect for their many contributions throughout history. It also reinforced and encouraged the full flowering of what he had called the "genius of women" in his earlier encyclical, *Mulieris Dignitatem*, On the Dignity of Women. In terms of thanks, the great pontiff wrote, "The church desires to give thanks to the most holy Trinity for the 'mystery of woman' and for every woman—for all that constitutes the eternal measure of her feminine dignity, for the 'great works of God,' which throughout human history have been accomplished in and through her."³

To consecrated women, he offered special thanks: "Following the example of the greatest of women, the mother of Jesus Christ, the incarnate Word, you open yourselves with obedience and fidelity to the gift of God's love. You help the church and all mankind to experience a 'spousal' relationship to God, one which magnificently expresses the fellowship which God wishes to establish with His creatures."⁴ Here we see a bridge between St. Albert's time and our own, between two great lovers of the Virgin Mary and two great lovers of all of those women who would specifically dedicate their lives to following the Blessed Mother's footsteps through vows of poverty, obedience, and chastity in the service of Christ.

In this chapter, we'll look at some of St. Albert's interactions with the women of his day: especially religious women, to whom he was a special friend and benefactor. Our great man of science was always most willing to visit religious sisters, to hear their confessions, to preach and inspire them, and even to help found their convents. These godly women held St. Albert in great esteem, as we'll soon see when we examine yet more Albertine legends.

DOMINIC'S DAUGHTERS

Oral tradition holds that the very first Dominicans to reach Germany found there groups of holy women, some of them living in poverty and even wearing religious habits. These groups the Dominicans began to organize into convents, blessed with the monetary assistance of wealthy young ladies and widows who wanted to join the order and devote their lives to God. They would. By the time of Albert's death, the German province he once governed would be blessed with 65 convents—more than in the rest of the provinces combined—full of Dominican sisters wearing the white woolen tunic, cloak, long scapular, and small veil.

And so that characteristic Dominican call to learning and teaching became the vocation of women as well, and with Albert's help their influence spread far beyond Germany and far beyond the 13th century. I know this well myself, having spent the first nine years of my formal education under the auspices of those black-and-white habited Dominican Sisters of Springfield, Illinois, whose mother house is but a mile from where I write. Nearly 800 years after Albert's time, I can assure you that Dominican Sisters are still sharing the fruits of their contemplation!

ALBERT THE GREAT AND THE GREAT-NIECE OF THE EMPEROR

One of the earliest stories of Albert's beneficent dealings with a convent (and another example of his work as a peacemaker) dates from 1237, during the time he was being called around Germany to found new convent schools. Take note how this incident prefigures one in the life of a young St. Thomas.

One Iolanda, daughter of Count Vianden, himself the nephew of the emperor of Constantinople, had decided to become a religious, taking the habit at the convent of Marienthal, founded in 1232. Her family was sore-vexed at this 18-year-old's swift decision, so much so that they stormed the convent and brought her back home to the family castle. For help in judging their fate they called—well, who else would they call, if not the wise young professor already known far and wide for his unsurpassed wisdom and justice? When St. Albert arrived at the castle, young Iolanda fell at his feet and implored him to take her vows on the spot. Albert deliberated for a time and was overcome by her genuine zeal, recognizing her true call to the religious life. He advised her family to her return her to the convent, and to her great joy they did. Later, after her father had died in a Crusade, her mother became a religious at Marienthal as well, and a brother became a Dominican friar.

THE LADIES OF PARADISE

Albert's travels through Europe found him in many convents, where no doubt he touched sisters' lives with his impromptu preaching and teaching. He also had a hand in founding one of the most famous Dominican convents. In the year 1252, John of Wildhausen, the fourth general of the order, conceived the idea of a convent in the city of Soest within the Diocese of Cologne. The friars proceeded to preach and solicit to build this holy haven, and donations came in aplenty—not only in money but in property and even in lives. Wealthy and prominent citizens sought admittance for their wives and daughters. According to early historian Rodolph, "the women and young maidens inhabited a common dwelling, and commenced to climb the mountains of perfection,"[5] but they lacked a common rule of life. Who could provide them with the structure and holy inspiration to continue their ascent? You guessed it. Answering the call of the Bishop of Osnabruck, Provincial Albert arrived in 1259, instructing the holy women in the Rule of St. Augustine and the constitutions of the Order of Preachers.

A poignant story is told of the night of their formal entrance into the convent, like a parade of wise virgins carrying their lamps for Christ. Proceeding from outside the walls of what was then called Alvoldinghausen, clothed in poor garments and accompanied by local clergy, laity, and many noble knights, the women gathered in the sanctuary of the convent in which they would dwell for the rest of their days. From the altar St. Albert instructed them in the proper behaviors of their rule, reminding them of their vows of poverty and obedience, and exhorting them toward cordial love for one another, the community, and God.

Together the sisters chanted, "I have despised the kingdom of the world and all earthly attire for the fervent love of my Lord Jesus." Albert bestowed his Benediction upon them and closed the doors that would forever separate them from the world outside.

Albert was also given the authority to allow the daughters of the Chevalier Arnold to transfer from the Benedictine order into this new convent. Arnold himself would don the Dominican habit and run the worldly affairs of the convent, while his wife Cunigond would be elected its first superior. Arnold declared that henceforth, the convent would be known as "Paradise," a joyous prelude to Heaven on Earth.

Though uplifted by their ardent zeal, Albert also left them with sober advice for the future. For instance, being well aware of the problems experienced by some convents in Italy and France, he advised that they be careful not to admit too many recruits or those who were not well-suited to the rigors of the demanding monastic mode of life. He also advised against erecting new buildings too quickly. The convent did thrive and grow, at just the right speed, and years later, Bishop Albert of Ratisbon would fittingly return to consecrate their new church.

St. Albert in Paradise

Albert's love for his sisters in Christ can also be seen in his will. As the bishop of Ratisbon, St. Albert had been allowed to retain some measure of wealth and property, which he likely used in part to supply books for his work and his order. In his last will and testament, from January 1278, he also included behests to two convents of sisters.

Further, among the Albertine legends are two apparitions to sisters. The first story involves a Cistercian abbess who, after Albert's death, had prayed for him with her sisters in gratitude for the repeated acts of kindness he had shared with them during his lifetime. After a brief sleep one morning, the abbess awoke to see Albert standing ready to address the people in the church, but his feet were not on the ground. When she exclaimed aloud her fear that Brother Albert would fall, she was told that he need never fall again. Albert began a sermon, stating, "Full of grace and truth," and then adding, "Such are the marvels my eyes now behold."[6]

An early biographer, Peter of Prussia, also cites an apparition that appeared to St. Mechltilde of Helpode in the 1290s. It was taken from the *Little Treatise on Spiritual Graces* that Henry of Halle put together from the saint's *Revelations*. She reports a glorious apparition of two great saints approaching the throne of "the King of the mansion of the saints." Escorted by angels bearing candlesticks of great beauty, the two saintly figures wore garments with bright letters of gold that exuded a fragrant aroma. Those words represented their knowledge of the divinity and humanity of Jesus Christ, which they taught in their works. They were presented by the angels to the king as participators in the gifts of the Cherubim and Seraphim (the highest of the angels in Heaven). They had become "like saints" because "they sought during their passing life to resemble them in everything by their virtues and knowledge." They would indeed be officially canonized as saints one day, the first in 1323 and the second in 1931. They were St. Thomas Aquinas and his beloved mentor, St. Albert the Great.

Within 50 years of their deaths, the two great doctors would also appear in another paradise—Dante Alighieri's epic poem *Paradiso*. We'll hear Dante let them speak for themselves in Chapter 15. But first in the coming chapter we examine how St. Albert, this ardent lover of his spiritual sisters, loved even more dearly their spiritual Spouse.

GREAT IDEA #13: HAPPINESS

> Albert reminds his reader that he who does not experi-
> ence satisfaction from doing the virtuous thing does not
> yet possess the virtues (*sed non ut iusti et casti*).[7]

Before St. Albert's time, theologians rarely addressed the question of earthly happiness. But the fruits of Albert's careful contemplation included practical prescriptions for attaining not only paradise in the hereafter but happiness in the here and now. Both considerations are focused on our *ends* or goals as human beings. Borrowing from Aristotle's ethical writings, Albert noted that earthly happiness is a natural end or goal state. Whether a person seeks money or fame or achievement or earthly pleasure, his intention is always that those things will provide the means to the end, which is happiness.

But in order to be happy, we must pursue the goals that are truly good for us as human beings. Our desires must be guided by reason, and this is achieved through the development of the sundry natural virtues—prudence, justice, temperance, fortitude, and all of their allied moral and intellectual virtues. When we have trained ourselves to apply these virtues, even in difficult situations or when involving self-restraint or deprivation, even virtuous actions themselves provide a certain pleasure or satisfaction.

In his understanding of our final and eternal ends, building with his human reason on the revelation that his faith provided him, St. Albert the Great offered a vision of happiness immeasurably higher than any imagined by even that wisest of the Greeks. This ultimate happiness is beyond both the reach of reason and faith because when we will not need to believe in great things unseen we will come to see in the light of glory (*lumen gloriae*), the ultimate good (*primum bonum*) of the Beatific Vision.

Chapter 14

Thorough Theologian

Almost, we can say, like a first Adam on the earth, in the middle of thirteenth century Albert of Cologne began to look at the world around him with a completely fresh gaze. In his commentary on Matthew's Gospel he wrote: "The whole world is theology for us because the heavens proclaim the glory of God."

—Paul Murray, O.P.[1]

One should bear in mind the difference between the contemplation of the faithful Catholics and that of pagan philosophers, for the contemplation of the philosophers is for the perfection of the contemplator himself, and consequently it is confined to the intellect and their aims in it is intellectual knowledge. But the contemplation of the Saints, and of Catholics, is for the love of him, that is of the God they are contemplating.

—St. Albert the Great[2]

S T. ALBERT has been described as a scientist by temperament, a philosopher by choice, and a theologian by mood. When a natural explanation appeared to explain an observable phenomenon or process, such as the operation of our senses, Albert did not feel the need to interject a supernatural cause. Thus for Albert there was never conflict between science and religion, faith and reason, the material and the spiritual realms; indeed, as we saw earlier, for him "the whole world was theology," because "the heavens proclaim the glory of God." And as Albert made clear in his *On Physics*: "Whatever is known by two ways instead of one is better grasped; hence what is known by faith and reason is better understood than that which is known only by faith."[3]

FORMA MENTIS: AD MAJOREM DEI GLORIAM

In our examination of Albert's science and philosophy, we have hardly begun to ascend the first step of the towering ladder of theology that Albert had erected toward Heaven. The form of his mind, the framework and end of all of his intellectual and practical endeavors, was always and ever to glorify the God who lovingly created and sustains the whole of his creation. Even his strictly theological works make up a formidable literary corpus. He commented on every book of the Bible. We have already taken the briefest glimpse at his loving Marian writings. Albert also wrote books about the Mass and the Eucharist, considered by some to have no equal, not even in the writings of the towering St. Thomas. Albert too wrote a *Summa Theologica*, an advanced and stupendous compendium of nearly all things theological—left unfinished, according to some, when the master saw that his student's work had exceeded his own in its clarity, focus, and sublimity.

St. Thomas's *Summa Theologica* has been called by some a physically tangible gift of the Holy Spirit—a gift of understanding, knowledge, and wisdom that we can actually hold in our hands. So too are St. Albert's writings true and lasting spiritual gifts brought to us through a great saint who, though so thoroughly grounded in reason, stood ever open to the illuminating graces of God.

REASON'S REASONS

In St. Albert's theologically perilous times, though, some were teaching not that truths can be known in multiple ways but that there were *two* truths—that one thing might be "true" according to faith, and its contrary could also be "true" according to reason. Armed with the rigorous logic and metaphysics of Aristotle, Albert and Thomas cut through the contradictory nonsense and firmly established in Catholic doctrine the vital role, and limits, of reason.

Recall how some prominent men of his day, and even some within the Dominican order, feared ancient pagan wisdom as a threat to Christian dogma. Albert, of course, could not have disagreed more fully or more vehemently. By championing valid methods of science, of reasoning and argumentation, of the understanding of causation, of essence and existence, of substance and accident, of permanence and change, and other categories of fundamental importance to our understanding of creation and its Maker, Albert demonstrated that natural truths of pagan philosophy could never be an enemy of the supernatural truths of Christian faith, since all truth has the same Author. Thus it has been said that Albert, along with St. Thomas, "baptized" Aristotle.

Unlike many scientists today who, unlike Albert, make no effort to master philosophy, reason did not lead Aristotle away from God. On the contrary, though he had not the benefit of divine revelation, reason alone led the Father of Logic to see that a "Prime Mover" must exist.[4] That's why Aristotle called metaphysics the "divine science"—a science fit for the gods and one that leads man to God. From Aristotle we also obtain excellent though incomplete insight on the nature of the human mind and soul: other parts of the vast edifice of wisdom that waited 1,600 years for Sts. Albert and Thomas to lay its last precious stones.

Albert introduced profound philosophical considerations into a natural theology that speaks to us of God from what we can glean from nature, using the reasoning powers He gave us. But reason is not the *only* way to know and the *natural* is not the only realm. Albert understood more deeply than any man, perhaps save one, that although philosophy is a most powerful servant, it is a servant only; it is the handmaiden of theology, which seeks to know not only wisdom but wisdom's source.

Revelation Revealed

Reason can climb only so high: it can bring us to Heaven's gate, but it can't open the doors to reveal the wonders that lie inside. Reason can point to God and show us that he is One, Unique, Uncaused, Creator, Eternal, Omniscient, Omnipotent, Purposeful, All-loving, and more, but it cannot show us He is Three, that His Holy Spirit proceeds from the Father and Son through love, or that His Word willingly became flesh for us. And that is why our professor, our reader of ancient learned texts and writer of his own, loved even more dearly the scriptures and the theological patrimony of the ancient Church Fathers.

Albert's love and mastery of scripture show through in his every theological work, including the commentaries he wrote on many books of the Bible. His most famous of these was his *Commentary on St. Luke's Gospel*, in which he relates incidents from his own life and times to show how the messages of the gospel are immediately relevant to all people in every age. His lectures to the papal court on the gospel of St. John were famous throughout the Church, and some say that he habitually recited the Psalter (all the psalms) *every day*!

It should come as no surprise to hear that St. Albert was an amazingly multifaceted theologian. This man who brought logic, metaphysics, epistemology, philosophical psychology, natural law, and virtue ethics to the service of theology, who plumbed the depths of Sacred Scripture, also left a lasting legacy of spiritual theology. He would serve as a great inspiration to later great German mystics, influencing the likes of his junior contemporary, student, and fellow Dominican Meister Eckhart and, two centuries later, a fellow resident of Cologne and author of the incomparable *Imitation of Christ*, Thomas à Kempis.

Perhaps St. Albert's most significant purely spiritual work is one that he may not have written in its entirety. The beautifully simple, though profoundly moving, *De Adhaerendo Deo* (On Cleaving to God), which has been called a worthy companion to Thomas à Kempis's *Imitation*, is about "cleaving freely, confidently, nakedly, and firmly to God alone . . . since the goal of Christian perfection is the love by which we cleave to God."[5] It has been attributed to St. Albert, but modern scholars point to references within its pages that suggest it was penned in not the 13th century but the 15th. Still, others note that of the book's 17 chapters, the first 9 hang together in a way that the last 7 do not, raising the possibility that Albert wrote those chapters and the other were later accretions.

Whatever the truth may be, this book undeniably abounds in sources and concepts dear to Albert, such as the following:

- Aristotle—the senses, imagination, and intellect
- St. Augustine—the parts of the human soul (reason, memory, and will) mirroring the Trinity
- The Neoplatonic philosopher Dionysius (or "pseudo-Dionysus")—the *via negativa,* or negative way to God[6]

Whether he wrote it in whole or in part or not at all, the book is truly Albertine, reflective of his theological contribution to the Church.

I can picture the older Albert (whom we shall meet two chapters down the road), finally withdrawn from the cares of the world, focusing his all upon God, as his thirst for the knowledge of God in his intellect gives way to a desire for the eternal union with God through infusion of supernatural charity in his soul. For as we read in *De Adhaerendo Deo,* saintly contemplation "crosses over into the will through love," and further, "it is not the spiritual that comes first, but the natural (1 Corinthians 15:46), so one must proceed by the usual order of things, from active work to the quiet of contemplation, and from moral virtues to spiritual and contemplative realities."[7] St. Albert, whose life abounded in active fruits of his intellectual contemplation and who wrote as no one save St. Thomas on those moral virtues, would at the end be free to focus his contemplation on God alone, fired by that highest spiritual virtue of charity.

There we have Albert at the end of his life, approaching his final *telos*, his ultimate goal, the Beatific Vision. Later we will revisit

Albert's last days on Earth, but now we must look more closely at the road Albert took to get there, at that scientific theology that Albert never forgot must serve a practical end: the salvation of souls.

The Art of Prayer

Although he was the consummate man of science, St. Albert knew that there is also an *art* to almost anything we do (recall that art is related to *artifice* and *artificial*, to the act of making and the things man makes from the materials supplied by nature). St. Albert's great master Aristotle even listed art as a *virtue* of the practical intellect, something that we can hone and perfect. For Albert the memory master, the highest end of the art of memory is to recall the words, commandments, precepts, and principles of God and His Church, so that we may live according to the guidance of divine prudence.

For Albert the theologian, there is also an *art of prayer*: specific methods gleaned from scripture and the Church Fathers that we can use to shape our outer environments and our inner dispositions so as to cleave to God through prayer most fully and intimately. Let us turn first to the advice of the prudent preacher on preparing for prayer.

Here St. Albert's two key dimensions are *time* (remote time leading up to prayer and at immediate time at the moment of prayer) and *location* (in exterior bodily acts and in movements within the soul).

As for the remote preparation for prayer within our own souls, we must start by *purifying our conscience*, because scripture advises us that God will hear us when our own hearts do not reprove us (James 4:8). We must next *humble our minds* because God hears the cries of the humble and answers their petitions (James 4:10). Third, we must *forgive anyone who has injured us*, as Jesus advised us in His own prayer, so that God may forgive us our trespasses as we have forgiven those who have trespassed against us (Matt. 6:12–15).

So then, with purified consciences, humbled minds, and forgiving hearts, we may next direct our gaze outside ourselves and make the equally vital external preparations. If we would seek to adhere to

St. Albert on Preparation for Prayer

	Interior preparation	Exterior preparation
Remote preparation	1. Purification of conscience	1. Fulfillment of God's Commandments
	2. Humbling of the mind	2. Reconciliation with anyone we've offended
	3. Forgiveness of injuries	3. Fasting and almsgiving
Immediate preparation	1. Personal recollection	1. Place
	2. Focusing attention on God	2. Appearance
	3. Stirring up devotion to God	3. Gesture

Note: Adapted from text of Albert's *A Treatise on the Manner of Praying*, as appearing in Thomas C. McCongile and Phyllis Zagano's *The Dominican Tradition* (Collegeville, MN: Liturgical Press, 2006), 16–18.

God in prayer, we must first *obey the commandments* He has given us. Albert cites St. Isidore here, noting, "If we do what the Lord commands, we will without doubt obtain what we ask for." Next, heeding the advice we find in Matthew 5:23–24, we must *actively reconcile* with any brother or sister we have offended or who holds something against us, leaving our offering of prayer upon the altar until we have been reconciled. Finally, we prepare for a prayerful state by almsgiving and fasting, which move us away from worldly and fleshly concerns and ready our spirits for God.

We move now to the moment leading to the actual commencement of prayer. Now we must first practice *personal recollection*, in which we gather our wide-ranging thoughts and emotions and put them at God's service. Here Albert applies a beautiful mystical interpretation of Matthew 6:6, "But when you pray, go into your room and shut the door and pray to your Father who is in secret." Entering the room, he says, is the personal recollection within our hearts and shutting the door is the maintenance of that recollected state during prayer.

Next we most *cast off all carnal and worldly concerns*, focusing the "pure eye of the heart" on nothing but God. Here Albert bids us recall the prefatory prayer of the Mass, in which the priest proclaims, "Lift up your hearts," and we reply, "We lift them up to the Lord." And then, with purified consciences, humbled minds, forgiving hearts, recollected thoughts, and attention purely on God, we must *kindle the fires of our devotion to God Himself*. Albert tells us one effective means is to consider our own miserable state in contrast with God's boundless mercy and love.

With our intellects and wills now oriented toward God, we reach the three last external preparations. The first regards the actual physical *place* of our prayer. Albert notes that depending on the context, prayer can be done standing, sitting, or even lying down, but he reminds us that public prayer, such as at Mass, should always observe the forms and postures prescribed by the Church. As for *appearance*, Albert first notes that a humble and abject demeanor is in order, for it fosters reverence for God. Furthermore, when we pray we should reverently employ bodily postures and gestures—genuflecting, lifting of hands, beating of the breast, raising and lowering of the eyes, and more. Albert was keenly aware that God had crafted us as mind-body unities and that we cleave to Him most fully when we seek that union with *all* that there is of us: in our heads, in our hearts, and indeed in our very sinews.

St. Albert on the Mass and the Eucharist

We have seen how our youthful theologian waxed eloquent in his *Mariale*, singing the praises of the Mother of God. Now, near the end of his days, our most learned and seasoned man of God turned the light of his towering reason on two of the central mysteries of the Faith: the Eucharist and the Holy Sacrifice of the Mass. In those works composed near the close of his life, St. Albert, "no longer appears a mere mortal, but as one filled with the Holy Ghost and fed with celestial bread: he might be likened to the beloved disciple reposing on the breast of Jesus and contemplating at leisure those awful mysteries."[8]

In the spirit of true scholasticism Albert sought to find the reasons behind all the liturgical practices and prayers within the Mass. To do this, he borrowed heavily from the ancient Church Fathers and dipped deep into the well of his own immense knowledge of scripture and Church history.

For example, Albert mused on the reasons why the *Kyrie* is sung in Greek, rather than in Latin:

1. "Because it was in Greece that the most sublime wisdom flourished, as it is said in the Epistle to the Corinthians: 'The Jews requires signs, and the Greeks seek after wisdom.'"
2. Because of their observance of laws and natural justice, "for as the Jew recognized this justice of the Gospel through faith in the justice of the Mosaic law, so also the Greek discovered the justice of the Gospel through faith in natural justice."
3. Because the majority of the New Testament had been written in Greek and the first seven churches were founded in the parts of Asia Minor called Greece.
4. Because the Faith came to the Latins from Greece, whence Sts. Peter and Paul had traveled first. The words of the

Kyrie recall that the Greeks were the first of the Gentiles
to receive from Paul and Barnabas the grace of salvation
(Acts 13). "That this same grace was borne from Greece
into the West, we preserve in the words and syllables which
that people first used to implore the mercy of God."[9]

Albert goes on to describe the development and regulation of the
liturgy through the first four Church councils—Constantinople, Nice,
Antioch, and Ephesus—noting, for example, that Pope Sergius had
decreed that the Host be divided into three parts. The first was con-
sumed by the priest to represent the union of the Church Triumphant
with Christ, the second was put into the chalice to symbolize the
Church Militant "floating in a sea of tribulation,"[10] and the third was
saved until the end of Mass to symbolize the Church Suffering, which
would unite with Christ only in the last days. But in his day, Albert
concludes, "as the faith of Christian people is now grown weak, the
Priest immediately consumes the parts which represent the Church
militant and the Church suffering."

To Albert all the symbols, prayers, gestures, and practices of
the liturgy spoke of immeasurable depth and beauty, and he knew
that the light of reason could only penetrate them so far—that they
must remain essentially mysteries. Near the end of his sermon on
the "sacrament of the altar," he wrote, "A host of things which the
human mind cannot grasp still remain hidden in the secrets of God; it
behoves us to leave them to the light of the Holy Ghost, to the fervour
of piety, without dissertating longer on them."[11]

In my next time for prayer, I'll follow our great saint's instructions on proper preparation, both inside and out. And my prayers will
include a petition for more of this great saint's theological writings to
be published in English. I believe that if St. Albert, loving theologian,
would speak to us today, his wish for us would match one that in past
days he proclaimed at the time of Communion: "May the peace of
Christ and the Church superabound in your souls!"[12] In the next chapter, we'll see how a love of Christ, the Church, his order, and his most

gifted student led this peacemaking man of love to don the spiritual armor of a charging knight: an undaunted champion of what is right!

GREAT IDEA #14: THE VIRTUE OF RELIGION

Here's a bit of a paradox. Sts. Albert and Thomas, two of the most profound religious thinkers in all of history, note that annexed or related virtues of the principal cardinal moral virtues of prudence, justice, temperance, and fortitude somehow fall short of the full embodiment of the cardinal virtue to which they are related. Now, religion is considered an annexed part or related virtue to the virtue of justice. How then does what we owe God fall short of the mark of natural justice? How could religion be a lesser virtue?

Justice involves rendering to others their rightful due. We saw this already in another virtue related to justice, that of the piety that we owe in particular to our parents and our country. Religion, however, relates directly to what we owe to *God*, and it only falls short in relation to justice because we can never repay God what is rightfully due to Him! He has given us our very existence and there is no way we can repay Him *in equal measure*.

Nonetheless, through the development of the virtue of religion within ourselves, we can train ourselves to honor and serve God with all our heart, mind, soul, and strength, through both exterior and interior acts. St. Albert's own virtue of religion is evident in every chapter of his life (and, I hope, in every chapter of this book). For those who would care to learn more deeply about religion *as a virtue*, until St. Albert's works are someday completely available in English, I refer you to his pupil Thomas's *Summa Theologica*, second part of the second part, questions 81–100, wherein he devotes over a hundred pages to the ways we can do our best to render justice unto God.

Chapter 15

Charging Champion

His most illustrious pupil was Thomas Aquinas, whose
genius he perceived and proclaimed: and all his life
Albert held Thomas in a close friendship of holiness and
learning; he stoutly defended his teaching when Thomas
was dead, and always paid tribute to his greatness.

—Pope Pius XI[1]

I was a sheep of the sacred flock which Dominic leads
through pastures fair, wherein he who turns not aside
finds abundant food. He who stands on my right hand
nearest me was my Brother and master, he is Albert of
Cologne, and I am Thomas of Aquin.

—Dante, *Paradiso, Canto X*

WE have seen how St. Albert was the consummate peacemaker,
thanks to the abundance of his charity and wisdom. But when
the occasion called, though it was late in his life, our holy Teutonic
warrior, "with the shoulders of a giant,"[2] would gladly don his Christian armor, with his pen as his lance and his wit as his sword, and
charge forward as truth's irresistible champion. We'll examine the
knightly St. Albert's attacks and defenses in a few of his most memorable tournaments. In the first, the honor of his brothers was at stake, in
the second, that of his writings, and in the third, that of his spiritual son.

SECULAR VERSUS RELIGIOUS: A STRANGELY MODERN JOUST

The sons of St. Francis and St. Dominic who stirred the embers of the fires of Christendom in the early 13th century, leading to the real fireworks that followed, were mendicants who had cast off the *stabilitis loci*—the vow of stability within a local monastery—that characterized earlier monastic orders. We have seen that St. Dominic emphasized early on that learning must underlie preaching, which led them to use the University of Paris as a training ground for their holy, educated evangelists. By the mid-12th century, Dominicans and Franciscans had occupied doctor's chairs there for decades.

But during those decades the presence of those friars was gradually generating animosity from the secular professors in Paris (and in other universities in France and Italy as well) and also from some local bishops who resented their independence (the orders and friars received their authority to teach, preach, and hear confessions not directly from the local bishop but from the pope himself). It's likely too that the often-wealthy professors and clerics were scandalized (or perhaps shamed) by the contrast between their worldliness and the simplicity of the mendicants.

That holy demeanor of the Dominicans and Franciscans, not to mention their ardor for learning, drew many a promising student away from the many pedants of the day, as well as from intellectual fads such as the near-pantheism of Abelard and the "monopsychism," "unity of the intellect," or common intellectual soul proposed in the writings of Averroes. As the acerbic Oxford Franciscan and medieval scientist Roger Bacon observed, only partly tongue in cheek, for 40 years secular scholars had neglected philosophy and theology.[3]

Enter into this scene a professor named William of St. Armor, "an able and eloquent teacher, an artistic peddler of backstairs gossip, especially against the Mendicants . . . generally called the most artful liar of his time, adept at spreading half-truths."[4] St. Armor had written a book titled *The Perils of These Latter Times*, in which he attacked the religious friars' authority to teach and hear confessions and even argued that because they lived on alms and did not do manual labor, they could not be saved! This controversy grew to threaten the entire future of the Dominicans and Franciscans, and when St. Armor arrived in Rome to plead and to stir up his cause, it was brought to the attention of Pope Alexander IV.

The pope determined to investigate the allegations, and the friars responded with a delegation to the papal court, residing in Anagni at the time. The delegation included the Franciscans St. Bonaventure and Thomas of York, and the young Dominican doctor, St. Thomas Aquinas. Its leader was Albert the Great. They all spoke powerfully in defense of the work of the mendicant orders, none more so than St. Albert. The early biographer James of Soest notes that "such was the eloquence of Albert's reply and his words so telling that all present were filled with amazement and glorified God who had chosen such a man to defend his Order from evil tongues."[5]

Albert laid out an explanation of the nature of the mendicant orders, a defense of their existence, and a case for their unique, fully faithful role in spreading the gospel. He explained, for example, that being a "mendicant" did not imply literal begging for alms (*mendicus* literally meaning "beggar" or "poor man")—as if Dominicans spent their time roaming the streets looking for handouts—but rather eschewing money and personal property and living on the voluntary generosity of others. They did not have to make a living off their physical labor, as did some orders of monks, because their *intellectual* labors were valid contributions to the welfare of the Church. As physical work was to the Benedictines a kind of prayer, for the Dominicans it was *study*. The friar was not the monk's successor or competitor but his complement. These, and other of Albert's well-considered clarifications, helped secure the future of the Dominicans, Franciscans, and later kindred orders, even unto our time. So effective, in fact, was Albert's defense that St. Armor's book was condemned in the papal bull *Quasi Lingnum Vitae* of October 18, 1256, and its author was banished from Paris.

DON'T GRATE THE GREAT!

So much of Albert's youth was spent in spreading great truths among those who recognized their greatness. Alas, in his later years he would spend more energy defending those truths from the ravages of ignorance, distortion, and perhaps at times malice. Let's move now to April 1271. A series of dubitable propositions on things theological had been causing for some time a considerable stir in the Dominican *studium* of Venice, and even a letter from Thomas Aquinas in reply to the Venetian lector had not quelled the controversy. We don't know the substance of the disputed questions themselves, though Weisheipl notes they were *not* related to certain problematic propositions out of the University of Paris that we will visit shortly.

This we do know, however: in his efforts to resolve this dispute, Dominican General John of Vercelli sent a list of 43 controversial propositions to the three most learned Dominican theologians of the day. Separate letters went out to Thomas Aquinas, still in Paris, to Albert the Great in Cologne, and to Robert Kilwarby, then serving as the English provincial, in London. They were bidden to answer as quickly as possible with their opinions of each proposition according to these three criteria: (1) Did the Fathers of the Church proclaim it? (2) Would the Fathers have held such a proposition, or does the respondent himself hold it? (3) If the respondent does not hold the opinion himself, could such a doctrine or opinion nonetheless be tolerated without harm to the Faith?

True to form, St. Thomas replied with short, sweet, and relevant answers to each question. Kilwarby, Weisheipl tells us, "was lengthy and magisterial" and, foreboding of future conflict to come, revealed "many differences from the other two."[6] St. Albert, though in doctrinal accord with St. Thomas, was actually quite irritated and annoyed by many of the questions, describing them as "fatuous," "stupid," "fantastic," and "inquisitive." He then concluded that he answered the questions only out of love and reverence for the master general, for he was "going blind with old age" and "would rather spend the rest of his days in prayer than in answering silly questions."[7]

So why was Albert so sorely vexed? Recall that more than 20 years prior he had helped craft the very methods of his order's formal studies, so he likely felt he had covered all that ground long before. In his response to the general, Albert cited his own writings, including *De Causis*, *Metaphysics*, *Ethics*, and *De Animalibus*. How could the young Dominican lectors be so ignorant so soon of the work of their own great master?

Knowledge and wisdom must be won anew with each generation. The great saints can set for the young great examples and lay up for them true treasures in their words and their deeds, but it is up to each new generation to seek and claim those treasures. Albert's rebuke was also a lesson to his brothers that it is the responsibility of teachers to unearth and share those treasures—if they are going to wear the Dominican habit!

When the Dead Praise the Living

By March of 1274, St. Albert was in his well into his seventies and at home in relative leisure, lecturing at his beloved convent in Cologne, when he was invited by Pope Gregory X to the Second Council of Lyons, to convene in May of that year. The Council would deliberate, among other things, a possible *rapprochement* of the schism with the Greek churches. An ailing St. Thomas Aquinas also heeded the papal summons and started out from Naples to Lyons. A legend is told that at some point on the day of March 7, 1274, Master Albert, still at Cologne, began to weep. When his brethren asked him why, he replied, "Thomas, my son in Christ, the bright luminary of the Church, passes at this very moment from the world to his Lord!"[8]

And it was so. While riding to Lyons the Angelic Doctor was knocked from his mount by a low-lying tree branch. Not long after the accident, at the Cistercian Abbey at Fossonova, St. Thomas passed from this world at the age of 49, perhaps from a brain hematoma incurred in the collision. We don't know for sure the cause of his death, but we do know of many of its effects.

Though Albert, nearing the end of his own days, may well have longed to be rejoined with Thomas in paradise, he was certainly not one to let loss and sadness deter him from his lifelong goal of bringing souls to Christ. Events would soon come to pass that would lead our ancient warrior once more to don Christian armor to defend the doctrines of his beloved spiritual son, doctrines that could help bring untold numbers to Christ for centuries to come.

On December 10, 1270, Stephen Tempier, bishop of Paris, had condemned 13 theses derived from the Muslim philosopher Averroes's interpretations of the writings of Aristotle. Some theologians saw these popular but heretical ideas as proof that Aristotle contradicted core truths of the Catholic faith. But Albert and Thomas saw how Averroes had in fact distorted Aristotle and were diligent in providing their own commentaries on the writings of the Stagirite. They sought to show what he truly said, to make clear the value his natural wisdom had for the Church and also to point out where and why he was sometimes in error.

For some, however, including the former Dominican provincial (and now archbishop of Canterbury) Robert Kilwarby, Albert and Thomas were no better than the Averroists and were likewise seen as threats to the Faith, especially to the extent that they dared to challenge the prevailing ideas of St. Augustine. (Both great saints greatly honored and widely quoted St. Augustine, but they recognized that like Aristotle—and themselves—he could not be entirely free of error on philosophical and psychological issues.)

In January of 1277, with the controversy still hot, Pope John XXI wrote to Bishop Tempier, ordering to find out what specific errors were being promulgated, by whom, and in which writings. Bishop Tempier then solicited input from multiple theologians and gathered a list of 219 propositions said to be contrary to the Faith. This was done largely to combat the growth of heretical Averroist ideas, promulgated in part by Sigar of Brabant, but the list also included

16 philosophical positions that were clearly compatible with the writings of St. Thomas Aquinas. And indeed, the bishop appeared well aware of the connection with Thomas, since it was on March 7, 1277, the third anniversary of Thomas's death, that he took it upon himself to condemn the ragtag list of propositions rather than refer them to the pope.

So what were the 16 "Thomistic" propositions? I refer you to Weisheipl's masterful biography on St. Thomas for the full list, some, perhaps all of which will seem abstruse and overnuanced to the modern reader. Here's one that Archbishop Kilwarby condemned only 11 days later, namely, "that the vegetative, sensitive, and intellective [souls] constitute one simple form."[9] St. Thomas, it seems, had a very logical and consistent interpretation of what was called "the unicity of substantial form in every composite."[10]

Clear as mud? All right, then, so what's an example of a "composite"? How about you or me? Human beings are composites of body and soul. Our bodies are made of matter, and the "form" that gives us life and makes us human beings is the "soul." The "unicity" refers to the "oneness" of the two. We are not beings of two natures put together but rather the union of two forms as a single nature. Sts. Albert and Thomas knew that this idea was Aristotelian, and they believed that it was true as well and in perfect harmony with the Catholic faith.

Archbishop Kilwarby and others of his frame of mind, believing erroneously that they had St. Augustine behind them, taught that matter can be "informed" by *multiple* forms; that, for example, we possess vegetative, sensitive, *and* intellectual souls, rather than one human intellectual soul (possessing within it both vegetative and sensitive powers). Further, they believed in the existence of a *forma corporeitatis*, or corporal form of the body alone, that had to be present before other forms. In fact they argued that this was necessary "to ensure the identity of Christ's body on the cross and in the tomb."[11] St. Thomas, in reply, had argued that "even the dead body of Christ was always united to the Divine Person hypostatically, and therefore the same body."[12]

This may seem to us like splitting hairs, but to Albert's keen mind it was anything but, and such false condemnations were enough to revive our aging philosophical and theological champion. Summoning the fortitude to walk hundreds of miles, and the humility to put his learned reputation on the line in defense of another, St. Albert charged slowly but surely to Paris, the city where he sat in the Dominican chair of theology 30 years prior, to meet Bishop Tempier's challenges head on. There he began his speech to the learned professors by saying, "What a glory it is for one who is living to be praised by those who are dead." He went on to portray St. Thomas as the one who truly lived, while his accusers in orthodoxy were covered in shades of death through their ignorance and ill-will. He defended the orthodoxy of Thomas's writings, as well as his personal sanctity, offering to defend them both before an assemblage of competent men.

Albert's words produced no retractions in Paris or Oxford, but they were not spent in vain. He returned to Cologne and pored over in sequence all the voluminous works of his late friend and student. After his renewed studies, awed and revitalized by the magnificence of Thomas's achievements, Albert invoked another assembly of Dominicans at Cologne. There he staged another impassioned plea on behalf of St. Thomas, who "by his writings labored for all to the end of the world, and that henceforth all others would work in vain."[13]

The sons of St. Dominic took to heart the humble words of their greatest living scholar. After a general chapter meeting in Milan in 1278, two lectors would be dispatched to the English province to inquire who was *"in scandalum ordinis"*—scandalizing the order by promoting disrespect for the writings of Friar Thomas. (Kilwarby by that time had been named cardinal bishop of Porto and Santa Rufina and was residing in Rome.) Meanwhile, back in Paris, by 1279 the Dominican general chapter had stated that attacks against Thomas or his writings would not be tolerated within the order, and by 1286 every Dominican friar in Paris was ordered to teach the lessons of Master Thomas.

Through the subsequent centuries, pope after pope would join Albert in singing the praises of the *person* and the *doctrines* of

Thomas Aquinas (Saint Thomas Aquinas as of 1323 and Doctor of the Church as of 1567). Pope John Paul II said in our time that "the Church has been justified in consistently proposing St. Thomas as a master of thought and a model of the right way to do theology."[14] The *Catechism of the Catholic Church* abounds in references to the writings of St. Thomas to explicate our faith. St. Thomas's writings on natural law would bear great fruit in the understanding and defense of human rights in the modern nations of the West, and indeed throughout the world in international law. Even Martin Luther King would cite the writings of St. Thomas Aquinas in his condemnations of injustice. St. Thomas truly left behind him epochal, world-changing legacies of achievement in philosophy, theology, and law.

But those Thomistic riches might have been buried right along with Thomas were it not for the tireless championing by his great friend. Albert would outlive his beloved "dumb ox" by six years, and despite his thinning hair, dimming eyesight, and stooped shoulders, Thomas's intellectual and spiritual father also became the first and the foremost Thomist.

GREAT IDEA #15: APOLOGETICS

Always be prepared to make a defense to anyone who calls you to account for the hope that is in you, yet do it with gentleness and reverence; and keep your conscience clear, so that, when you are abused, those who revile your good behavior in Christ may be put to shame.

—1 Peter 3:15–16

We are able to defend the Faith when we know what we believe and are able to reasons for it—when we know both the "whats" and the "whys" of our religion.

A truly great defender of the Faith, St. Albert knew that learning the "whats" calls upon both natural intellectual virtue and the Holy Spirit's gift of *understanding*. And the patron of the sciences he knew as well that to comprehend the "whys" of our beliefs, we must employ both natural intellectual virtue and the Holy Spirit's gift of *science*, that virtue by which we know causes and effects—how the truths of the Faith bear upon one another.

Finally, in order to know that the Faith is more worthy of understanding and knowing than anything else in the universe, St. Albert would teach us that we need both natural intellectual virtue and the Holy Spirit's gift of *wisdom*, that overarching "head of the other sciences," the gift that "makes the soul flourish."[15]

So then, to build our own capacities to defend our Faith, there are few greater sources than Professor Albert's own theological and philosophical writings, and to hone our capacities to do so with gentleness, reverence, and clear conscience, there are few better examples than Saint Albert's life.

Chapter 16

Cherished Child

But in order that thou mayest know that it is to my
bounty, and not to the exertion of thy own mind, that
thou art indebted for this immense knowledge, thou shalt
be completely stripped of it before thy death.

—The Virgin Mary to St. Albert[1]

Archbishop Sigfried came to the Dominican Convent
to visit, as usual, his dear Albert, the friend of God and
man, and knocking at the door of his cell, called out,
"Albert, are you there?" The venerable Master did not
open the door, but merely answered: "Albert is no longer
here; he was here once upon a time."

—Rodolph of Nijmegem[2]

TO keep both mind and body fit into old age, the best advice is
"use it or lose it," that is, stay as mentally and physically active
as possible. Now, it's arguable that St. Albert was among the most, if
not *the* most intellectually active person in all of recorded history! As
for his mind, he "used it" like no other, producing a volume of written
material on a vast array of subjects while teaching into his seventies,
and, as we have seen, leading an exceptionally busy practical life in
an abundance of roles. As for physical exercise, we must not forget
his strict practice (and enforcement) of the Dominican rule of travel
by foot.

It shouldn't surprise us, then, that Albert maintained his intellectual prowess even into his eighth decade. His last will and testament,

from January 1278—only three years prior to his death and placing him somewhere between 72 and 85 years of age—declared him sound of mind, and there is no indication it was ever contested. If that was so, however, things changed quickly thereafter. Albert's close friend Bartholomew of Lucca reports that for nearly three years prior to his death Albert had lost full use of his memory.

MEMORY MASTER FINALLY FORGETS

Some pious legends report that Albert's memory loss was sudden, occurring right in the middle of a lecture. When he realized what had happened, Albert proceeded to explain in great detail the apparition of his youth, his appeal to the Virgin Mary for help with his studies, and her promise that he would possess unequalled learning but would lose his memory not long before death. Some report that he lost his grasp of philosophical principles while retaining his memory of the texts of Aristotle and the scriptures. Even as his mind softened, he was believed to have continued to lecture at Cologne until close to the time of his death and to continue to say Mass.

In his last few years, St. Albert also became increasingly reclusive, saying little and hardly visiting with his brethren and others who came to call. The incident described by biographer Rodolph at this chapter's start is a poignant illustration. He notes that the archbishop of Cologne, when greeted by Albert during a visit in the saint's twilight years, heaved a great sigh and burst into tears, proclaiming to the others that Albert's words were true: "Albert was once here, but he is here no longer."

In those last days it was as if Albert's lifelong fascination with and understanding of the temporal things of creation could no longer suffice: he would desire now only their Creator. The boots that had carried Albert all over medieval Europe now haltingly trod the paths of the garden cloister, their wearer silenced and turned inward to prayer and meditation. Those boots also carried him daily to the site he had selected for the final resting place of his body, as he prayerfully and peacefully prepared for the imminent and inevitable day of his death. His spirit strove solely to cleave to God.

THE GREAT SHALL BE THE LEAST

It is a sad but fitting and sometimes a beautiful thing to observe a great human being, blessed with a vigorous life full of blessings for others, suffer gracefully the physical and mental decline that precede death. In my teens I observed another great champion of the Faith ascend to the papacy at 58, brimming over with exceptional physical vigor and mental sublimity and full of plans to traverse and transform the world. And for the next 26 years he did both, despite the growing physical debilitation that his Parkinson's disease would bring him.

Less than three years after Karol Wojtyla became Pope John Paul II, a 68-year-old man was elected president of the United States, and he would join with John Paul II in advancing human freedom and dignity by hastening the demise of atheistic Soviet Communism. He too suffered great mental decline in his last years, battling Alzheimer's dementia before passing from this world in 2004, less than a year before John Paul II.

Sometimes I would wonder what former President Reagan and his family were going through as they watched world's most powerful secular leader gradually lose the ability even to recognize his friends. (This is perhaps especially intriguing and moving to me since I did my doctoral internship and dissertation research with Alzheimer's patients in the 1990s.) If it is a sad and sobering experience to see a loved one lose his mental faculties, it must be a thing of terrible awe to watch a truly great thinker or man of action reduced to a vacant and feeble state of dementia.

What was it like to watch the great St. Albert in those last years of his life?

Modern research indicates that certain kinds of memory capacity are usually the first mental capacities to be lost, as they were in Albert's case. This most vulnerable form of memory is called "secondary memory," and most specifically, is the ability to retain and recall newly acquired information after a delay. In my own research, for example, I found that very early in the course of Alzheimer's, when most mental abilities are reasonably well-preserved, patients can perform essentially as well as nondemented individuals, matched for age, on immediate memory tasks such as repeating back a string of digits in order. Introduce a brief delay of even a few minutes, however, and information that the healthy elderly individual can hold onto has slipped forever from the memory of the patient with dementia. Further, information that a healthy elderly person cannot recall might come back to him with a hint, or he might recognize a word he has seen when it appears on a list or in a sentence, but not so for the victim of a dementia. We know that this phenomenon is actually linked to early destruction of brain cells in the hippocampus of the temporal lobes, which are essential for the formation and retention of new memories.

The person early in the throes of dementia may also retain a much better memory for information learned long ago than for that encountered recently. Recall how St. Albert reportedly could recall the texts of Aristotle and the scripture and retained the ability to say the Mass. Might he have been suffering from Alzheimer's dementia? It's possible—the likelihood of contracting Alzheimer's does greatly increase late in life. Some accounts, however, also mention that his memory loss was sudden, which is not typical of Alzheimer's.

Sudden losses of memory and other mental capacities often arise from other causes, often of cardiovascular origin, such as strokes or smaller blood flow events called transient ischemic attacks. Head injuries present another possibility. Some have speculated that St. Thomas Aquinas may have been enfeebled by a stroke before suffering a later brain injury from striking his head on a tree limb. President Reagan's own medical history was complicated by his being thrown from a horse and suffering a subdural brain bleed five years before he was diagnosed with Alzheimer's disease.

The pious story of Mary's prophecy notwithstanding, other reliable reports suggest a more gradual decline rather than a sudden loss of mental powers. We know that even in his last few years Albert composed a will and took part in certain ecclesial projects. Long after he resigned his bishopric of Ratisbon, he was called on repeatedly to assist in episcopal functions throughout Germany. Still, whatever its cause and however its onset, St. Albert's mental powers and physical vigor went into marked decline in the years immediately preceding his death. The man who knew all there was to know still lived, but his knowledge was passing away.

A World That Has Lost Its Minds

St. Albert's last moments in Cologne, and on Earth, came in the twilight hours on Friday, November 15, 1280. Clothed in the habit of the Order of Preachers, seated in a large wooden chair in his cell and surrounded by his brothers, St. Albert whispered that it had been a good thing to be a Dominican, and he serenely left to meet his Maker and his Lady.

In an essay from the 1930s, Robert Kloseterman, O.P. noted, "Time has proved that great men never appear singly in history; they are always closely associated with kindred spirits who labor zealously and perseveringly for the realization of their leader's ideals."[3] Not only do great men live together; sometimes they die together. In a space of six years and four months, a century blessed with great saintly thinkers like none other before or since lost *three* of the greatest theological minds who would all later be proclaimed Doctors of the Church: the Angelic Doctor, St. Thomas Aquinas; the Seraphic Doctor, St. Bonaventure; and now their senior comrade and champion, the Universal Doctor, St. Albert the Great.

A Saint for All the Aged

Albert did not leave the earth in an instant of glory, like the martyrs, nor while still in the prime of life as Thomas and Bonaventure had, while still in the prime of his earthly life. The brilliant light that radiated from his soul dimmed before its spark was gone. In his last years, his finely honed intellectual powers, which belong to the immortal soul but depend on mortal flesh to function in this world, began to degenerate. The body that tramped all over Europe on missions of every sort now creaked, stooped, and shuffled, as Albert prayed quietly within a humble cell and waited with hope to meet his loving Maker. But Albert was magnanimous to the end, for true greatness of soul includes the humility to recognize that by ourselves we are small and helpless, but through Christ who strengthens us we can do all things.

GREAT IDEA #16: NATURAL LAW

The end of law, then, as envisaged by Albert is primarily the growth of virtue in people. Prohibitions against evil are only incidentally (per accidens) the end of law; they are made only when there are impediments or obstacles to goodness.[4]

St. Thomas Aquinas is usually cited, along with Aristotle and the Stoics, as a monumental figure in the development of the theory of natural law and its relation to both human reason and virtue. Here too, though, as in so many other areas, it was Albert who broke the ground upon which Thomas would build.

Theologians before Albert tended to give precedence to laws over rights and virtues. We were virtuous, then, when we obeyed laws. Albert, however, championed the concept of natural right as an inborn, innate *habitus*, impressed *within* our very human souls; indeed, in Albert's own words, "written by the finger of God and inserted in the human heart."[5] This natural law within our hearts is an inclination of nature toward the good, and "natural right is the light of morals (*lumen morum*) impressed on us according to the nature of reason."[6]

It is up to us, then, to strive to build virtue within our souls by living according to the dictates of our God-given reason. Those of us who do will require no legal statutes to coerce us to act rightly and justly.

Conclusion

The Undisputed
Universal Doctor

Albertus Magnus has studied and described the entire
cosmos from stones to stars.

—Josef Wimmer[1]

To him belongs this great honor, that (excepting
St. Thomas) there is scarcely another doctor of equal authority, whether in philosophy, theology, or the interpretation of Scripture. It would be an endless task to recount
all that Albert had done for the increase of theological
science. Indeed, it was to theology that the whole trend
of his mind was inevitably directed.

—Pope Pius XI[2]

S T. ALBERT the Great's teaching is "universal" in many senses of
the term. In one sense, Albert did present us with an amazingly
broad array of facts and theories about the universe itself, covering
"the entire cosmos from stones to stars."

But universal also means "applicable to all persons, times, and
situations." Do you seek to understand the perennial philosophy? Go
to Albert. Do you want to love Mother Mary more deeply? Go to
Albert. Do you wish to grow in awe and wonder of the Eucharist?
Go to Albert. Do you wish to improve your memory, to retain in your
mind the lessons you learn? Go to Albert. Do you strive to grow in
holiness through prayer despite your many worldly duties, to be a

peacemaker among your friends, to instill order within your family, to build intellectual, moral, theological virtue, to develop every day a greater appreciation of the vastness of the universe and of the incomparable goodness of its Creator? Go then to Albert.

I certainly do not stand alone in such lofty and universal praise of our great-souled man. As we conclude this study then, we'll survey key events that intervened in the 651 years between his death and his canonization, we'll peruse some of the written treasures he's left us, and we'll consider some ways that we, as St. Albert's intellectual and spiritual heirs, his modern-day students and benefactors, can heed the call to make his universal lessons known throughout our world today.

FROM COLOGNE TO ROME IN SIX AND ONE-HALF CENTURIES

In the years following Albert's death, stories of apparitions and miracles abounded. We examined two apparitions to holy sisters in Chapter 13. Here we'll consider two more. It is told that one night shortly after Albert's death, he appeared to his friend and confessor of a dozen years, Gottfried of Duisberg. Appearing in a cloud of light and wearing pontifical robes, Albert told him the human mind cannot begin to fathom the wonders God had shown him. He explained that the rays of light projecting from his miter signified the glories that had been bestowed on him, and the precious stones that covered his robe were the books on Sacred Scripture that he had published to make the Divine Wisdom known and to lead the ignorant to knowledge of God. He said also that God had accorded to Albert's prayers the deliverance of 6,000 souls from Purgatory.

Another legend tells of another apparition sometime after 1297 to a teaching master named Dietrich of Freiburg, who had known Albert during his life. One night a recently deceased woman appeared to Dietrich and told of her eternal happiness in sight of the Holy Trinity. Dietrich asked her about Albert and she told of his unspeakable bliss.

Albert had been laid to rest in a wooden casket in the very choir of the Dominican chapel at Cologne that Albert's own financial generosity had made possible. The tomb faced the altar at which he had so often celebrated the sacrifice of the Mass. It was covered with a simple stone slab protruding a few inches from the floor, and it bore this inscription:

In the year of our Lord 1280, on the fifteenth day of November, died the Venerable Brother Albert, former Bishop of the Church of Ratisbon of the Order of Preachers and Master in Theology. May He rest in peace. Amen.[3]

Albert's tomb quickly drew pilgrims and there were stories of miracles attributed to his intercession. After three years his tomb was opened for relocation to another part of the church, and Albert's body was incorrupt, exuded a pleasant fragrance, and had turned within the casket in a face-down position, in which Albert was known to like to pray.[4]

Sometime before 1297 the archbishop of Cologne presented the church with a stained glass window depicting him kneeling at the feet of St. Albert in his full pontifical garb. In 1323 Albert's name was among three submitted to Pope John XXII for possible canonization. Another was Raymond of Pennafort, but the saint recognized that year was none other than Albert's intellectual and spiritual son, Thomas Aquinas. In 1480, the miraculous cure of a Dominican at Cologne was attributed to Albert's intercession. Two years later, Pope Sixtus IV canonized St. Bonaventure.

On January 11, 1482, at the request of Pope Sixtus IV, St. Albert's relics were relocated to a more resplendent tomb. When the vault was opened, in the presence of Archbishop Herman of Cologne, along with Dominican Master General Salvius Casetta and German Provincial James Sturbach, again a fragrant odor was noted. The wooden coffin lid had rotted away from 200 years of dampness, and yet, when the moist earth that had accumulated was carefully scraped away, they beheld a body well-preserved and with very little damage. The head and limbs were all intact, the eyes were in their sockets, the flesh was on his chin, and part of his beard and one ear were still visible. His pontifical vestments were intact, with his miter showing some signs of wear, a copper ring on a finger of his left hand, and his right hand holding the crosier. The ribbon attached to a relic of the true Cross among other relics was still attached. The Dominican master general removed the right arm as a holy relic, which he presented to Pope Sixtus IV, who in turn gave it to the Dominicans of Bologna. The rest of Albert's remains were enclosed in a glass case for public view.

The next year, Pope Innocent VIII gave permission to the priories of Cologne and Ratisbon to erect altars in Albert's honor and to observe his feast. In 1487, Peter of Prussia wrote a biography of Albert and composed a liturgical office sanctioned by Innocent VIII for use in the Dominican convents of Cologne and Ratisbon. Yet during the tumultuous times of the next century and more, little progress was made in the cause for Albert's sainthood.

From 1542 to 1616, on the heels of the Reformation, the city of Lauingen was under Protestant rule. Still, in 1601 the general chapter of the Dominicans again took up the cause and in 1616 the bishop of Ratisbon petitioned the pope to introduce the great Albert's feast into Ratisbon's cathedral. By 1670 the feast had been extended to the entire Dominican order, but there was still no canonization.

Another hundred years passed, more tumult reigned, and in 1799 Napoleon's troops invaded the lands of the Rhine, driving the Dominicans of Cologne from their convent home. In a mere two hours, these small men of war destroyed the church and the choir of the great man of peace. In 1804 Albert's relics were transferred to the Church of St. Andrew, where they remain to this day.

A half-century later there was peace, and Pope Pius IX extended Albert's feast to the diocese of Cologne, to other German dioceses, and then, quite fittingly, to Paris. Still, though more than 500 years had passed since the canonization of Albert's pupil, the master's day had not come. By then Albert had been popularly called a "Doctor of the Church" for nearly 200 years, but when the Dominicans petitioned Rome for him to be officially recognized as such, they were told of the unlikelihood that any religious order, with the exception of the ancient order of the Benedictines, could expect to have more than one of its sons named as Doctor. Once again Albert's star was obscured by the only one that has ever shone brighter.

Nonetheless, German bishops, exhibiting that enduring perseverance that Albert himself connected with the virtue of fortitude, petitioned at the Vatican Council of 1870 that Albert be declared Doctor. This however, could not be done for a man who was not yet canonized. So on the 600th anniversary of his death in 1880, the German bishops petitioned Rome for Albert's canonization and from 1890 to 1899 published new editions of his works.

Enter now certain prominent Dominicans of the early 20th century, who join with the German bishops to promote Albert's cause. A new edition of Rodolf of Nymegen's *Legends of the Blessed Albert*, a book indispensable to subsequent biographers, appears. In 1930 the postulator of the Order of Preachers stands up for the cause and on June 22, 1931, the Congregation of Rites begins its inquiries. On December 16, 1931, Pope Pius XI issues his decretal letter *In Thesauris Sapiente* and at long last, 651 years after his death, the man called great in his own lifetime would be recognized as St. Albert the Great, Universal Doctor of the Catholic Church.

A mere ten years later, when the greatest of modern scientists would turn their talents to the creation of weapons of mass destruction, inaugurating an age of explosive (both literally and figuratively) scientific advances, the world found itself in dire need of scientists as full of wisdom and charity as of technical know-how. It was not a moment too soon, then, when on December 16, 1941, yet another pious pope, Pope Pius XII (himself a third-order Dominican) declared the St. Albert the patron saint of natural scientists.

ALBERTUS MAGNUS: OPERA OMNIA

Despite Albert's unparalleled success in the active life, his wearing so many hats, from the Dominican's woolen hooded cowl to the bishop's ornamented miter, in the words of Pope Pius XI, "All this life of business and activity was as nothing compared to the immense labor of his studies and his many learned works, in which are gloriously displayed the force and acuteness of his genius, the fullness and depth of his mind, the overflowing wealth of his genius, the overflowing wealth of his erudition, and his indefatigable zeal in defending the faith."[5] Listing or summarizing Albert's works is no easy task. Few men in history were so prolific. Furthermore, some works attributed to Albert (such as *On Cleaving to God*) are of questionable authenticity. Charlatans tried to capitalize on Albert's great fame, writing books of alchemy and the occult in his name. We must remember too that Albert was always the scholar and author, even while playing his roles as provincial, bishop, peacemaker, crusader, and more. As he traveled from convent to convent throughout Europe he left behind a trail of texts as Paul had left his trail of tents. The collection, authentication, and translation of these works has been an ongoing operation for centuries.

Albert's writings can be categorized in a number of ways. One way is to separate the works in which he provided commentaries on others' writings (especially those of Aristotle), in which the interjection of his own views was relatively minimal, and those that reflect Albert's own independent reflections.

Another important way to categorize Albert's writings is by general subject matter. He wrote, for example, at least 35 scientific works, including *de Vegetabilus* and *de Animalibus*, the latter being considered the pinnacle of knowledge on animals produced in medieval times and the former earning him acclaim as the only scientific botanist in a period of 2,000 years.[6] Add to those scientific treatises Albert's 23 separate works of philosophy and scores of commentaries and monographs on scriptural and theological topics.

When, in 1651, the Dominican Peter Jammy of Lyons assembled the first edition of an *opera omnia*, a complete works of St. Albert the Great, it comprised 21 folio volumes. In 1890, when August Borgnet published his complete edition in Paris, there were 38. (As we saw, the appearance of these volumes is one thing that may have helped stoke the dormant cause for St. Albert's canonization.) Although a few books remain of questionable authenticity, the minimum number of genuine works from Albert's hands stands today at about 130.

As for the mostly academic writing generated throughout the world in response to Albert's inspiring genius, I refer readers of a scholarly bent to Irven Resnick and Kenneth Kitchell Jr.'s *Albert the Great: A Selectively Annotated Bibliography (1900–2000)*.[7] Published in 2004, this book cites more than 2,500 articles and books about St. Albert and his work! How does this square with my own lament of the relatively slim pickings of modern writings about St. Albert, especially compared to those about his great student, St. Thomas? This I will address in our final Great Ideas Box.

THE MAN IN THE MIDDLE

Dear reader, we have all but finished our story and I have a question to ask you before we go. Have you ever read G. K. Chesterton's biographies of St. Francis of Assisi and St. Thomas Aquinas?[8] In a certain sense, if you have I shudder, since you could be drawing comparisons between these pages and those and wishing wistfully that Chesterton, not I, had taken his brush to the canvas of Great Albert's life.

Well, though Chesterton did not write such a biography of St. Albert, he addresses him admirably well within a few pages of his biography of St. Thomas. Though that book was meant to be a companion to his life of St. Francis, at its outset Chesterton admits that a more direct comparison would be between St. Francis and St. Dominic, contemporaries in time and cofounders of their brother orders of traveling preachers. St. Francis was born around 1181 and died in 1226, when St. Thomas was an infant. Thomas was really a man of the next generation, St. Francis's "nephew" as Chesterton put it. But let us consider a man born pretty darn near the middle of those dates, between the days of the first mendicants and the first Thomists. For time is surely the least important sense in which he is "in the middle."

Chesterton compares and contrasts as well the bodies of his two favorite saints. Picture the small and wiry Francis, a man of God and the world who could hardly sit still, and the lumbering Thomas, a large-framed man after Chesterton's own heart. (In Chesterton's own words, "The gown that could contain the colossal friar is not kept in stock."[9]) As full of activity as was the sinewy Francis, so was the placid and corpulent Thomas absorbed in deep thought.

Then there is the man in the middle—described as of medium height but "with the shoulders of a giant." Between St. Francis, the classic bodily "ectomorph," and Thomas, true "endomorph," stands the embodiment of a mighty manly "mesomorph," equipped both for bodily action and intellectual endeavor. There again then, right in the middle, is Albert.

Albert also stood boldly in the middle of heated battles, fearlessly defending faith and reason, the honor and rights of the mendicant orders, the wisdom of old Aristotle and young Aquinas. And still another middle stance occurs to me. No one was a greater lover of animals than St. Francis. And yet, what man literally wrote the book on animals, *De Animalibus*? Albert was a true lover of all God's creatures, enlightening and amusing us with stories from the forests and streams and skies, bristlingly alive with the multitude of God's lovely creatures as they run and swim and fly. St. Francis loved nature. St. Thomas loved books. St. Albert loved to write books about nature.

No man looked deeper into the nature of the angels than St. Thomas Aquinas. And yet, what man helped raise young Thomas to his unsurpassed heights of angelic intellect? Here again in the middle is St. Albert, that great-souled man with the shoulders of a giant, who, like a medieval Atlas, gladly bore the heavens on his shoulders, even while they stooped and sagged with age, so that all who came after him might get a closer look.

GREAT IDEA #17: SUGGESTED READING (AND WRITING)

It is unfortunately no easy task to recommend further reading in English, either by or on St. Albert the Great. Most of the older biographies, as I mentioned in the introduction, are fine but musty old tomes, out of print and hard to find. One notable exception is Sr. Mary Albert's *Albert the Great* (1948), reproduced in *Spirituality Today* in 1987 and available online.[10] Another is Sighart's massive (467 pages) and delightfully crafted classic *Albert the Great*, first published in 1876 and most lately reprinted in paperback in 2009 by BiblioBazaar. Those who might enjoy a modern, scholarly look at Albert's great contributions to virtue ethics and natural law are directed to Stanley B. Cunningham's *Reclaiming Moral Agency: The Moral Philosophy of Albert the Great* (2008).

And please see the endnotes of this book for several other great books about our great saint that I found helpful in crafting various chapters.

An easier task than recommending books by or about St. Albert to be *read* is recommending books about Albert that should be *written* and recommending books written by him that should be translated into English. I am not aware of any English translation of the Albertine opera omnia and can only hope and pray that one will someday exist.[11] In the meanwhile, for those who would care to study in greater depth the kinds of philosophical and theological ideas that Albert contemplated so deeply and shared so fruitfully, I direct you to the easily accessible works of the Universal Doctor's greatest student, particularly his *Summa Theologica* and *Summa Contra Gentiles*.

I have no doubt that the "first Thomist" himself would echo that recommendation.

Appendix 1

The Life and Times of St. Albert the Great

ca. 1200	Albert's birth (date uncertain scholars' opinions vary from 1193 to 1206)
1209	St. Francis' Order of Friars Minor approved by Pope Innocent III
1215	Fourth Lateran Council
1216	St. Dominic's Order of Friars Preachers Order approved by Pope Honorius III
1220	St. Dominic visits Padua
1221	Group of Friar-Preachers go from Paris to establish convent in Cologne
ca. 1223–29	Albert enters Dominican Order
ca. 1225	Birth of Thomas Aquinas
1233	Albert appointed lector of theology at Cologne Dominican priory
	Albert sent to organize convent school in Hildesheim
1235	Albert sent to organize convent school in Freiburg
ca. 1240	Albert sent to Paris to obtain doctorate in theology, begins *De Bono*
1244	Albert obtains doctorate in theology at the University of Paris
	Albert joined by Thomas Aquinas at Paris
1248	Albert appointed Regent at new *Studium Generale* in Cologne

1250	Albert helps draft the system of study for his order at Valenciennes
1254	Albert elected Provincial of his Order for Germany
1256	Albert goes to the papal court at Anagni to defend the mendicant orders against attack
	Pope Alexander IV retains Albert to lecture the Papal Court on theology
1257	Albert resigns as Provincial to focus on study and teaching
	Thomas and Bonaventure obtain doctorates in theology
1258	Albert noted to be back at Cologne
1260	Albert installed as Bishop of Ratisbon (Regensburg) by Pope Alexander IV
1262	Albert resigns his bishopric
1263	Albert commissioned to preach Crusade by Pope Urban IV
1264	Last document with Albert's name as Preacher of Crusade
1274	Thomas Aquinas dies on March 7
	Albert attends Second Council of Lyons at Pope Gregory X's invitation
1277	Albert defends the doctrines of Thomas at Paris
1278	Albert suffers a loss of memory, prepares his will
1280	Albert dies on November 15
1323	St. Thomas Aquinas canonized
1484	Albert's Feast Day among Dominicans approved by Pope Innocent VIII
1622	Albert beatified by Pope Gregory XV
1931	St. Albert canonized saint and declared Doctor of the Church by Pope Pius XI
1941	St. Albert declared Patron of Scientists by Pope Pius XII

Popes of Albert's Lifetime

- Innocent III (1198–1216)
- Honorius III (1216–27)
- Gregory IX (1227–41)
- Celestine IV (1241)
- Innocent IV (1243–54)
- Alexander IV (1254–61)
- Urban IV (1261–64)
- Clement IV (1265–68)
- Blessed Gregory X (1271–76)
- Blessed Innocent V (1276)
- Adrian V (1276)
- John XXI (1276–77)
- Nicholas III (1277–80)

Albert's Great Contemporaries

- Genghis Khan, First Mongol Emperor (1162–1227)
- St. Dominic Guzman (1170–1221)
- St. Francis of Assisi (ca. 1181–1226)
- Kublai Khan, Fifth of the Mongol Emperors (1215–94)
- Blessed Jordan of Saxony (1190–1237)
- Frederick II of Hohenstaufen, Holy Roman Emperor (1194–1250)
- St. Louis, King Louis IX of France (1214–70)
- Roger Bacon (ca. 1214–94)
- St. Bonaventure (1221–74)
- St. Thomas Aquinas (ca. 1225–74)
- Edward I, King of England (1239–1307)
- Marco Polo (1254–1324)
- Dante Alighieri (ca. 1265–1321)

Appendix 2

Prayer of Albert the Great at the End a Sermon

B E Thou Blessed, O Humanity of my Saviour, which was united to the Divinity in the womb of a Virgin Mother:

Be Thou Blessed, O sublime and eternal Divinity, who was pleased to come down to us under the veil of our flesh!

Be Thou forever Blessed who, by the power of the Holy Ghost, didst unite Thyself to virginal flesh!

I salute you also, O Mary, in whom the fullness of the Divinity dwelt!

I salute you in whom the fullness of the Holy Spirit dwelt!

May the most pure Humanity of the Son be equally Blessed, which, consecrated by the Father, was born of you!

I salute you, O unspotted virginity, now raised above all choirs of angels.

Rejoice, O Queen of Heaven, who didst merit to become the temple of the spotless Humanity of Christ!

Rejoice and be glad, O Spouse of the holy Patriarchs, who was deemed worthy to nourish and suckle at thy breast the Sacred Humanity.

I salute thee, ever blessed and fruitful virginity, which didst thou merit to obtain the fruit of life and the joys of eternal salvation.

Amen

Notes

PREFACE

1. A. D. Sertillanges, O.P., *The Intellectual Life: Its Spirit, Conditions, Methods* (Fort Collins, CO: Roman Catholic Books, 1946), 181.
2. St. Thomas Aquinas, *Summa Theologica*, IIae IIae Q. 129, a. 1. (New York: Christian Classics, 1981), 1722.
3. S. M. Albert, O.P., *Albert the Great* (Oxford: Blackfriars Publications, 1948).
4. S.T., IIae IIae Q. 129, a. 4, 1725
5. Albert, *Albert the Great*, 13–14; James A. Weisheipl, O.P., *Friar Thomas Aquino: His Life, Thought, and Work* (Garden City, NY: Doubleday, 1974).

INTRODUCTION

1. S. M. Albert, O.P., Albert the Great (Oxford: Blackfriars Publications, 1948).
2. Mary Jean Dorcy, O.P., *Master Albert: The Story of St. Albert the Great* (New York: Sheed & Ward, 1955).
3. See S. M. Albert, O.P., *Albert the Great* (Oxford: Blackfriars Publications, 1948); St. Albert's College ed., *Saint Albertus Magnus* (Racine, WI: Saint Catherine's Press, 1938); Thomas Schwertner, O.P., *St. Albert the Great* (New York: Bruce Publishing Co., 1932); Joachim Sighart, *Albert the Great: His Life and Scholastic Labours: From Original Documents* (Charleston, SC: Bibiliolife, 2009), a reprint of the public domain English translation of the French edition (London: R. Washbourne, 1876).
4. Luke 1:28.
5. 1 Corinthians 13:13.
6. Mark 28:30–31.

173

CHAPTER 1

1. Irven M. Resnick and Kenneth F. Kitchell Jr., trans., *Albert the Great: Questions Concerning Aristotle's* On Animals (Washington, DC: Catholic University of America Press, 2008), 351.

2. John Paul II, "Science and Faith in the Search for Truth" (paper presented to teachers and university students in Cologne Cathedral, November 15, 1980), http://www.its.caltech.edu/~nmcenter/sci-cp/sci80111.html.

3. B. R. Hergenhahn, *An Introduction to the History of Psychology*, 2nd ed. (Pacific Grove, CA: Brooks/Cole, 1992), 91–92.

4. Mary Jean Dorcy, O.P., *Master Albert: The Story of St. Albert the Great* (New York: Sheed & Ward, 1955), 8.

5. See Resnick and Kitchell, *Albert the Great.*

6. S. M. Albert, O.P., *Albert the Great* (Oxford: Blackfriars Publications, 1948), 68–69.

7. Resnick and Kitchell, *Albert the Great*, 337.

8. Here are a couple of quick examples, using reason alone, without consideration of faith and revelation. Science can show us how to build human clones, but we need *ethics*, a branch of philosophy, to determine if and when it is morally right to do so. Science can show how and if material bodies change in the course of evolution, but it takes *metaphysics* and *logic* to determine whether or not this has any implications for or against the existence of a spiritual soul.

9. Copies of St. Albert's scientific writings were found in the library of Christopher Columbus, annotated in the explorer's own hand.

10. Albert, *Albert the Great*, 39.

11. John Paul II, "Science and Faith in the Search of Truth."

12. I refer interested readers to my previous *Unearthing Your Ten Talents: A Thomistic Guide to Spiritual Growth Through the Virtues and the Gifts* (Manchester, NH: Sophia Institute Press, 2010), in which each of these intellectual virtues is addressed at chapter length.

CHAPTER 2

1. Thomas Schwertner, O.P., *St. Albert the Great* (New York: Bruce Publishing Co., 1932), 335.

2. Marianus Vetter, quoted in St. Albert's College ed., *Saint Albertus Magnus* (Racine, WI: Saint Catherine's Press, 1938), 17.

3. Joachim Sighart, *Albert the Great: His Life and Scholastic Labours: From Original Documents* (Charleston, SC: Bibiliolife, 2009), 3.

4. James A. Weisheipl, O.P., *Friar Thomas Aquino: His Life, Thought, and Work* (Garden City, NY: Doubleday, 1974), 39.

5. http://www.gbt.org/text/sayers.html.

6. Ibid.

7. This section borrows heavily from *Albert the Great* by Sighart, the only biographer I've found who thoroughly speculates on the details of Albert's likely education.

8. Ibid., 8.

9. Ibid., 9.

10. Seneca, *Letters from a Stoic* (New York: Penguin Books), Letter XI, 56.

11. Sighart, *Albert the Great*, 11.

12. See Cicero, *Rhetorica Ad Herennium* (Cambridge: Harvard University Press, 2004).

13. Sighart cites Flaminus, Leander, Jammy, and even later biographers. He also notes a similar apparition involving St. Dominic in which Cecelia and Catherine accompanied the Virgin Mary.

14. Jammy, cited in Sighart, *Albert the Great*, 24–25.

15. Schwertner, *St. Albert the Great*, 23.

16. St. Thomas Aquinas, *Summa Theologica*, IIae IIae Qs. 166 and 167 (New York: Christian Classics, 1981).

17. Cited in S.T. IIae IIae Q. 166.

CHAPTER 3

1. St. Thomas Aquinas, *Commentary on Aristotle's Nicomachean Ethics* (Notre Dame, IN: Dumb Ox Books, 1994), 366.

2. In St. Albert's College ed., *Saint Albertus Magnus* (Racine, WI: Saint Catherine's Press, 1938), 33.

3. Albert's name would be linked with a stone bridge traversing the Rhine built around that time. This would not be the last time he was labeled a great architect, though the structures most often attributed to him were churches.

4. Thomas Schwertner, O.P., *St. Albert the Great* (New York: Bruce Publishing Co., 1932), 34.

5. Walt Whitman, "Song of Myself," *Leaves of Grass*, section 47, http://en.wikiquote.org/wiki/Leaves_of_Grass.

6. St. Dennis was a late fifth- and early sixth-century theologian and Neoplatonic philosopher, also called Pseudo-Dionysius the Areopagite or Pseudo-Denys.

7. Joachim Sighart, *Albert the Great: His Life and Scholastic Labours: From Original Documents* (Charleston, SC: Bibiliolife, 2009), 71.

8. Schwertner, *St. Albert the Great,* 35.

9. James A. Weisheipl, O.P., *Friar Thomas Aquino: His Life, Thought, and Work* (Garden City, NY: Doubleday, 1974), 44.

10. S. M. Albert, O.P., *Albert the Great* (Oxford: Blackfriars Publications, 1948), 26.

11. See Matthew 19:21; Mark 10:21; and Luke 12:33, 18:22.

12. Schwertner, *St. Albert the Great,* 39.

CHAPTER 4

1. Irven M. Resnick and Kenneth F. Kitchell Jr., trans., *Albert the Great: Questions Concerning Aristotle's* On Animals (Washington, DC: Catholic University of America Press, 2008), 343.

2. Stanley B. Cunningham, *Reclaiming Moral Agency: The Moral Philosophy of Albert the Great* (Washington, DC: Catholic University of America Press, 2008), 198.

3. This translates as "Great philosopher . . . the greatest philosopher." Thomas Schwertner, O.P., *St. Albert the Great* (New York: Bruce Publishing Co., 1932), 251.

4. Jonathan Barnes, ed., *The Complete Works of Aristotle* (Princeton, NJ: Princeton University Press, 1984), 1552.

5. St. Thomas Aquinas, *Summa Theologica*, II, tr. i Q. IV (New York: Christian Classics, 1981).

6. On the particular issue of abstraction and illumination and the human intellect, I direct you to Leonard A. Kennedy's *Abstraction and Illumination in the Doctrine of St. Albert the Great* (Memphis, TN: General Books, 2010). This is a doctoral dissertation originally published in 1958. For a more detailed look at the nature of the soul and human psychology in the manner of Aristotle, Albert, and Aquinas, I refer you to my own *Unearthing Your Ten Talents: A Thomistic Guide to Spiritual Growth Through the Virtues and the Gifts* (Manchester, NH: Sophia Institute Press, 2009), as well as to Thomas Brennan's *Thomistic Psychology: A Philosophic Analysis of the Nature of Man* (New York: Macmillan, 1941), and, of course, to the writings of Aristotle and Sts. Albert and Thomas themselves as referenced in those books.

7. Cited in Cunningham, *Reclaiming Moral Agency*, 50.

8. Cunningham, *Reclaiming Moral Agency*, 161.

9. Ibid.

10. From Cicero's *De Iventione*, cited in Cunningham, *Reclaiming Moral Agency*, 188.

11. James 1:5.

12. Ibid., 3:17.

CHAPTER 5

1. Joachim Sighart, *Albert the Great: His Life and Scholastic Labours: From Original Documents* (Charleston, SC: Bibiliolife, 2009), 59.

2. From *De Bono* (*On the Good*), cited in Mary Carruthers, *The Book of Memory* (Cambridge: Cambridge University Press, 1990), 275.

3. Stanley B. Cunningham, *Reclaiming Moral Agency: The Moral Philosophy of Albert the Great* (Washington, DC: Catholic University of America Press, 2008), 36.

4. Cicero, *Rhetorica ad Herennium* (Cambridge, MA: Harvard University Press, 2004).

5. St. Thomas Aquinas, *Summa Theologica*, IIae IIae Q. 49, a. 1.

6. John 1:1.

7. John 3:3.

8. John 10:11.

9. In her delightful *The Book of Memory*, Mary Carruthers presents in an appendix St. Albert's meticulous analysis of the world's oldest memory improvement manual.

10. Proverbs 3:3.

11. *Catechism of the Catholic Church*, 1803; emphasis added.

CHAPTER 6

1. Thomas Schwertner, O.P., *St. Albert the Great* (New York: Bruce Publishing Co., 1932), 100.

2. Paul Murray, O.P., *The New Wine of Dominican Spirituality: A Drink Called Happiness* (London: Burns & Oates, 2008), 2.

3. Ibid., 147, 129, 135, 145, 170 (for the five bullet points).

4. Fr. Murray and others tell the story of one night in 1229 when a group of new Dominicans got the giggles and broke out into laughter during the Compline—nighttime prayers. They were reprimanded and told to stop by a more senior brother. Perhaps if you've been in a similar situation, you will understand how their laughter then grew all the louder. When the Compline was over, Blessed Jordan turned to them and told them to laugh to their heart's content, that they could be as merry as they pleased as new Dominicans "after breaking from the devil's thraldom." Murray, *New Wine*, 47–48.

5. Schwertner, *St. Albert the Great*, 19.

6. S. M. Albert, O.P., *Albert the Great* (Oxford: Blackfriars Publications, 1948), 13.

7. Cited in T. McGonigle and P. Zagano, *The Dominican Tradition* (Collegeville, MN: Liturgical Press, 2006), 18. I stand indebted to these authors for many insights in this section.

8. Matthew 5:8.

9. Matthew 5:3.

10. In the Dominican chapel in my own town, there are some traditional pews in the back for visitors. The sisters themselves sit in banks of seats that face inward toward each other to remind them that Christ also resides within us and within those across the aisle.

11. See, for example, Acts 10:3, 9; 16:23.

12. Both are among the 33 recognized "Doctors of the Church," renowned for their teachings on faith and morals. St. Albert has been named the "Universal Doctor," and St. Thomas the "Common Doctor" and "Angelic Doctor."

13. St. Thomas Aquinas, *Summa Theologica*, IIae IIae Q. 28. a. 4 (New York: Christian Classics, 1981).

14. Romans 14:17.

CHAPTER 7

1. St. Albert the Great, cited in St. Albert's College ed., *Saint Albertus Magnus* (Racine, WI: Saint Catherine's Press, 1938).

2. Ibid., 3.

3. Cf. Luke 2:46–47.

4. St. Thomas Aquinas, *Commentary on Aristotle's Nicomachean Ethics* (Notre Dame, IN: Dumb Ox Books, 1994), 366.

5. Abridged from Thomas Schwertner, O.P., *St. Albert the Great* (New York: Bruce Publishing Co., 1932), 57–58.

6. Ibid., 58.

7. St. Albert's College ed., *Saint Albertus Magnus*, 49.

8. S. M. Albert, O.P., *Albert the Great* (Oxford: Blackfriars Publications, 1948), 125.

9. Collected in *The Aquinas Catechism* (Manchester, NH: Sophia Institute Press, 2000).

10. St. Albert's College ed., *Saint Albertus Magnus*, 50.

11. 1 John 3:18.

12. S. M. Albert, O.P., *Albert the Great*, (Oxford: Blackfriars Publications, 1948), 124.

13. Ibid.

CHAPTER 8

1. Joachim Sighart, *Albert the Great: His Life and Scholastic Labours: From Original Documents* (Charleston, SC: Bibiliolife, 2009), 156.

2. Ibid., 152 (Albert's salutation in a letter to the Dominican houses of Germany).

3. Cf. Job 7:5. (This is just a play on words. Albert was clothed with the office of provincial at the Chapter at Worms. "Worms" actually derives from a Latinized version of an old Celtic word for a watery settlement, this one on the left bank of the Rhine in southwest Germany.)

4. St. Albert's College ed., *Saint Albertus Magnus* (Racine, WI: Saint Catherine's Press, 1938), 40.

5. Sighart, *Albert the Great*, 202.

6. Compare this to the harsh fates of Anias and Saphira in the presence of Peter after a similar crime (Acts 5:1–11).

7. Today, confession at least once yearly is the second of five "Precepts of the Church," being, in addition, (1) attending Mass on Sundays and Holy Days of Obligation, (3) receiving the Eucharist during Easter season, (4) observing prescribed days of fasting and abstinence, and (5) providing for the needs of the Church. (See the *Catechism of the Catholic Church*, nos. 2041–43.)

8. St. Albert's College ed., *Saint Albertus Magnus*, 42.

9. A most notable exception is found in the writings on spiritual friendship of St. Aelred of Rievlaux (1109–1166), of which it appears St. Albert was not aware.

10. Cited in Stanley B. Cunningham, *Reclaiming Moral Agency: The Moral Philosophy of Albert the Great* (Washington, DC: Catholic University of America Press, 2008), 243.

CHAPTER 9

1. S. M. Albert, O.P., *Albert the Great* (Oxford: Blackfriars Publications, 1948), 40.
2. Ibid., 41.
3. Ibid.
4. Ibid., 43.
5. Thomas Schwertner, O.P., *St. Albert the Great* (New York: Bruce Publishing Co., 1932), 107.
6. James 2:17.
7. St. Albert's College ed., *Saint Albertus Magnus* (Racine, WI: Saint Catherine's Press, 1938), 46–47.
8. As a bishop, Albert did sometimes travel with a pack animal, not to carry Bishop Albert but to carry his episcopal gear and his equally great treasures—his books.
9. Albert, *Albert the Great,* 40.

CHAPTER 10

1. Thomas Schwertner, O.P., *St. Albert the Great* (New York: Bruce Publishing Co., 1932), 78–79.
2. Joachim Sighart, *Albert the Great: His Life and Scholastic Labours: From Original Documents* (Charleston, SC: Bibiliolife, 2009), 166.
3. Ibid., 267.
4. S. M. Albert, O.P., *Albert the Great* (Oxford: Blackfriars Publications, 1948), 19.
5. Isaiah 11:2.

CHAPTER 11

1. Cited in Thomas Schwertner, O.P., *St. Albert the Great* (New York: Bruce Publishing Co., 1932), 350–51.
2. Paul Murray, O.P., *The New Wine of Dominican Spirituality: A Drink Called Happiness* (London: Burns & Oates, 2008), 123.

3. S. M. Albert, O.P., *Albert the Great* (Oxford: Blackfriars Publications, 1948), 52.

4. Joachim Sighart, *Albert the Great: His Life and Scholastic Labours: From Original Documents* (Charleston, SC: Bibiliolife, 2009), 168.

5. Lest you find it difficult to imagine your own bishop floating an explosive-laden barge down your local river, remember these were quarrelsome times when bishops were also secular and even military authorities.

6. The interdict was a papal penalty on a group or a region, akin to the excommunication of an individual. A city under interdict could be deprived of public services and Sacraments. Indeed, in a canon law instituted 100 years later, physical violence against a bishop was specified as offense warranting an automatic interdict.

7. St. Albert's College ed., *Saint Albertus Magnus* (Racine, WI: Saint Catherine's Press, 1938), 55. (I don't know about you, but for me, this stands as one fine and pithy example of St. Albert's eloquent practical wisdom.)

8. I Corinthians 13:13.

9. St. Thomas Aquinas, *Summa Theologica*, IIae IIae Q. 29, a. 1 (New York: Christian Classics, 1981).

CHAPTER 12

1. Cited in St. Albert's College ed., *Saint Albertus Magnus* (Racine, WI: Saint Catherine's Press, 1938), 19, from the *Mariale*.

2. Ibid., 21, from one of Albert's last sermons (perhaps he heard her beckoning).

3. From Song of Solomon 6:10.

4. From Rev. Robert J. Bushmiller, *The Maternity of Mary in the Mariology of St. Albert the Great* (diss., University of Fribourg, Switzerland, 1959), 27, citing from Albert's *De Naturi Boni* (On the Nature of the Good).

5. *Mariale*, Question 71. Cited in Buschmiller, *Maternity of Mary*, 96.

6. Cited in Buschmiller, *Maternity of Mary*, 30.

7. Ibid.

8. Cited in Buschmiller, *Maternity of Mary*, 92.

9. Ibid., 32.

10. Joachim Sighart, *His Life and Scholastic Labours: From Original Documents* (Charleston, SC: Bibiliolife, 2009), 331.

11. Pope Pius XII, "Defining the Dogma of the Assumption," Apostolic Constitution, November 1, 1980, cited in Cheryl Dickow, *Mary, Ever Virgin, Full of Grace: A Study of Papal Encyclicals on Mary* (Waterford, MI: Bezalel Books, 2010), 89.

12. *Mariale*, Question 29. Cited in Buschmiller, *Maternity of Mary*, 50.

13. S. Bittremieux, *S. Albertus Magnus Ecclesiae Doctor Praestentissimus Mariologus*, Eph. Theol. Lov. X 19330, 217–31, cited in Buschmiller, *Maternity of Mary*, 105.

14. Rudolphus De Noviomago, *Legenda Beati Magni*, I, p. 38, cited in Buschmiller, *Maternity of Mary*, 105.

CHAPTER 13

1. Rudolphus De Noviomago, *Legenda Beati Magni*, I, p. 38, cited in Robert J. Bushmiller, *The Maternity of Mary in the Mariology of St. Albert the Great* (diss., University of Friborg, Switzerland, 1959), 157.

2. Ibid., 160. Also cited in Thomas Schwertner, O.P., *St. Albert the Great* (New York: Bruce Publishing Co., 1932), 73–74.

3. Pope John Paul II, *Letter to Women for Bejing Conference*, section 1.

4. Ibid.

5. Joachim Sighart, *Albert the Great: His Life and Scholastic Labours: From Original Documents* (Charleston, SC: Bibiliolife, 2009), 159.

6. Thomas Schwertner, O.P., *St. Albert the Great* (New York: Bruce Publishing Co., 1932), 326; see also Sighart, *Albert the Great*, 425. (Both also recount the subsequent apparition of St. Mechtilde.)

7. Stanley B. Cunningham, *Reclaiming Moral Agency: The Moral Philosophy of Albert the Great* (Washington, DC: Catholic University of America Press, 2008), 262.

CHAPTER 14

1. Stanley B. Cunningham, *Reclaiming Moral Agency: The Moral Philosophy of Albert the Great* (Washington, DC: Catholic University of America Press, 2008), 93.

2. St. Albert the Great, *On Cleaving to God* (Indianapolis, IN: Lamp Post Books, 2008), 32–33.

3. Cited in Thomas Schwertner, O.P., *St. Albert the Great* (New York: Bruce Publishing Co., 1932), 277.

4. Compare Romans 1:19–20. St. Paul knew well that the natural wisdom of the Greeks had pointed them to God.

5. St. Albert the Great, *On Cleaving to God*, 9.

6. The *via negativa* is a method of speaking about God's perfection in terms of what we can say he is *not* (e.g., material, confined by time and space, etc.) rather than what he *is*, aiming at a mystical experience of God that transcends normal language and experience.

7. St. Albert the Great, *On Cleaving to God*, 38–39.

8. Cited in Joachim Sighart, *Albert the Great: His Life and Scholastic Labours: From Original Documents* (Charleston, SC: Bibiliolife, 2009), 302.

9. See Ibid., 304–6, for all quotations on the four reasons.

10. Ibid., 308.

11. Ibid., 311.

12. Ibid., 309.

CHAPTER 15

1. Decretal letter *In Thesauris Sapiente* of December 16, 1931.

2. Thomas Schwertner, O.P., *St. Albert the Great* (New York: Bruce Publishing Co., 1932), 202.

3. Cited in James A. Weisheipl, O.P., *Friar Thomas D'Aquino: His Life, Thought, and Work* (Garden City, NY: Doubleday, 1974), 81.

4. Schwertner, *St. Albert the Great*, 87.

5. Cited in S. M. Albert, O.P., *Albert the Great* (Oxford: Blackfriars Publications, 1948), 35.

6. James A. Weisheipl, O.P., *Friar Thomas Aquino: His Life, Thought, and Work* (Garden City, NY: Doubleday, 1974), 291.

7. James A. Weisheipl, O.P., *Albertus Magnus and the Sciences: Commemorative Essays* (Toronto: Pontifical Institute of Mediaeval Studies, 1980), 42.

8. Joachim Sighart, *Albert the Great: His Life and Scholastic Labours: From Original Documents* (Charleston, SC: Bibiliolife, 2009), 366.

9. Weisheipl, *Friar Thomas D'Aquino*, 337.

10. Ibid.

11. Ibid., 338.

12. Ibid.

13. Sighart, *Albert the Great*, 370.

14. Pope John Paul II, *Fides et Ratio*, "Faith and Reason," 1998 Encyclical (Vatican City: Vatican Publishing House, 1998), preamble.

15. Stanley B. Cunningham, *Reclaiming Moral Agency: The Moral Philosophy of Albert the Great* (Washington, DC: Catholic University of America Press, 2008), 265.

CHAPTER 16

1. Legend cited in Joachim Sighart, *Albert the Great: His Life and Scholastic Labours: From Original Documents* (Charleston, SC: Bibiliolife, 2009), 23.

2. Ibid., 416.

3. St. Albert's College ed., *Saint Albertus Magnus* (Racine, WI: Saint Catherine's Press, 1938), 59.

4. Stanley B. Cunningham, *Reclaiming Moral Agency: The Moral Philosophy of Albert the Great* (Washington, DC: Catholic University of America Press, 2008), 234.

5. Ibid.
6. Ibid., 236.

CONCLUSION

1. Cited in St. Albert's College ed., *Saint Albertus Magnus* (Racine, WI: Saint Catherine's Press, 1938), 38.

2. Cited in Thomas Schwertner, O.P., *St. Albert the Great* (New York: Bruce Publishing Co., 1932), 347.

3. Joachim Sighart, *Albert the Great: His Life and Scholastic Labours: From Original Documents* (Charleston, SC: Bibiliolife, 2009), 138.

4. Recall Albert's mention of praying while lying down from his recommendations for the preparation for prayer in chapter 14.

5. From *In Thesauris Sapiente*, reproduced in Schwertner, *St. Albert the Great*, 344.

6. Josef Wimmer, cited in St. Albert's College ed., *Saint Albertus Magnus*, 38.

7. See Irven Resnick and Kenneth Kitchell Jr., *Albert the Great: A Selectively Annotated Bibliography (1900–2000)* (Tempe: Arizona Center for Medieval and Renaissance Studies, 2004).

8. My copy is the doubly delightful G. K. Chesterton, *Saint Thomas Aquinas and Saint Francis of Assisi* (San Francisco: Ignatius, 1986).

9. Ibid., 19.

10. http://www.spiritualitytoday.org/spir2day/ag00.html.

11. I was pleased to discover while researching for this book that in Walter M. Miller Jr.'s 1959 science fiction novel *A Canticle for Leibowitz*, a cloister of monks in a desolate, postnuclear war future centuries hence exists to preserve and copy rare and precious texts (and especially works of science) from the greatest minds of the world before the war. Some of monks even serve the role of "memorizers." The name of this fictitious order is the Albertian Order of Leibowitz!

About the Author

KEVIN VOST, Psy.D. (b. 1961) has served as a college psychology professor, weightlifting instructor, fitness writer, Research Review Committee Member for American Mensa, lector for St. Agnes Catholic Church, and fast food fries and drink man (a few decades back). He is the author of *Memorize the Faith!*, *Fit for Eternal Life*, *Unearthing Your Ten Talents*, and *From Atheism to Catholicism*. A self-styled Thomistic Albertian, Dr. Vost lives with his wife and two sons in Springfield, IL. He welcomes your questions and comments at www.drvost.com.